BLOODY REVOLUTION

To Lucy, Ellen and Grace

BLOODY REVOLUTION
A JOURNEY INTO UK MMA

MICK BOWER

gutdor

Published by Gutdor Books

Gutdor Books
PO Box 755
ROTHERHAM
S60 9HW

gutdor@gmail.com

ISBN 978-0-9567764-0-2

Printed and bound in Great Britain by CPI

Cheers

To my editor Martin Smith for his advice and support.

To Martin Rhodes for the ace pic on the cover.

To the people who made this book possible: the fighters, trainers, promoters and fans who support the sport of mixed martial arts in the UK.

For notes, updates and supporting material please visit:

www.bloodyrevolution.wordpress.com

INVASION

UFC 70
M.E.N Arena , Manchester
April 21st 2007

- I...I thought he was dead.

I put my hands on Lucy's shoulders to reassure her. Slowly, her eyes opened wider to take in her surroundings. The expression on her face betrayed confusion giving way to embarrassment.

- In the cage. I thought he was dead.

This time she said it with more force, like an excuse. The lads who had helped her up started to snigger but stopped as soon as they saw the black look on my face. I was angry. Not at them- at the whole thing: the drip, drip, drip of sensationalist headlines, grandstanding politicians and general misinformation that led to this last utterance. OK, her brain may have been a little oxygen deprived but nevertheless, for a split second, the woman I live with thought I'd brought her to a public execution.

FLASHBACK: 15 MINUTES EARLIER

Normally, I arrive at a venue an hour or two early to pick up the gossip: who looks tight at the weight, has anyone been up to something different in the gym and are there any deals down the line that depend on certain results. Being wise before the event helps you to make sense of what unfolds in front of you and, in turn, makes it easier for you to explain it to your readers. Today was strictly pleasure and, when the sun is shining, there are few more pleasant things to do than sink a few pints outside the old boozers in Shambles Square.

Lucy didn't usually show much interest in my Saturday nights out, but she'd insisted on tagging along this time. The hype was obviously working. For weeks, billboards and radio ads had been trumpeting the coming of UFC 70: Nations Collide. The Ultimate Fighting Championship (UFC) had started out as a cable TV oddity. 14 years on it was billion dollar organisation that packed arenas, did huge numbers on pay per view and was the driving force behind the fully rounded sport of Mixed Martial Arts (MMA).

People love to watch fighting. It's the ultimate sport. By many measures, it's the only true sport- the definitive test of one man against another. Boxing had a clear run at supplying Joe Public with his fix of brutality, then everyone got greedy. 18 weight classes and an alphabet soup of belts devalued the whole concept of being a champion. Hideous mismatches, the obsession with unbeaten records and undercards packed with guys who weren't even household names in their own houses made boxing a parody of its former self. The gap in the market was filled by the UFC.

Success breeds success. Ad men were quick to spot the potential. The UFC's core audience are their dream demographic: 18-35 year old white males with a healthy disposable income. North America had been conquered and now Manchester was the first step on the road to world domination. The appeal was obvious. It was like a throwback to the golden age of boxing: a handful of weight divisions, a clear title picture, contenders forced to fight the best and, most importantly, well matched, exciting fights. Fans got cards that were stacked with quality from the main event down to the tenth feature. As a result, the fans would get into their seats early and watch the show from start to finish. But not tonight.

Timing was of the essence. Although Lucy appeared keen, I figured there was a chance her enthusiasm might start to flag. I decided that by skipping the bulk of the undercard, she was more likely to last out the night without getting bored.

We walked into the M.E.N.: straight into a wall of smoke and heat. The concourses were packed with eager fight fans who had decided that queuing for samosas and sucking cancer sticks were a better use of their time than watching the undercard. Due to our precarious financial situation at the time, we had opted for the bottom of the range £25 tickets. The first impression of the actual arena: HEAT. Unbearable heat. Probably due to its central location, the M.E.N. is steeply tiered to cram the maximum number of people into the smallest space possible. Great for atmosphere, but spare a thought for those of us who had seats in block 217- up in a far corner bang next to one of the six big screens. It's a sweltering day and you're within touching distance of the hot air pipes. The crowd downstairs are generating plenty of hot air; warm, stale air that makes life in the rafters even more uncomfortable. It started to dawn on me why there were so many refugees in the smoke room round the back.

I was delighted to get in for the final support bout; Terry Etim v Matt Grice. Terry was a rising star of the domestic scene. No doubt being from the North West had helped him get on the card, but he was a genuine prospect. The UFC weren't doing the lanky Scouser any favours though. Grice had an impressive wrestling pedigree and was unbeaten in his MMA career. From the crow's nest, you could follow the stand up, but you had to switch to the big screen to get a decent view of the ground work.

Terry tagged him early on then rushed in to follow up. He was too eager. Grice slammed him onto the deck and spent the next few minutes on top, dropping punch after elbow after punch onto Etim's head. There was sinking feeling in my gut. Nearby, people were watching through their fingers. Underneath a wrestler is the single worst situation a fighter can find himself in. Grice was in control. Terry was getting pounded.

Out of nowhere, Terry managed to scramble to his feet then attack with kicks and knees. Relieved cheers rang out. The pair clinched up. Etim locked a standing guillotine choke on. With Grice's head trapped under his left armpit, Terry applied maximum pressure to the throat with his forearm. Percentage wise, the standing guillotine is one of the least successful submissions in MMA. To execute a guillotine successfully, you want to pull guard (wrap your legs around your opponent) and fall back. This has its own risks. If his head pops out, it leaves you on the bottom and vulnerable. Terry stayed on his feet, biting on his gumshield as he strained for all he was worth. The guillotine takes as much out of the aggressor as the defender. The prolonged effort floods the shoulder muscles with lactic acid. If you don't score with the submission, your arms will feel like lead in the next stand up exchange and your opponent will pick you to pieces.

Grice's head slid out, drawing a groan from the partisan crowd. The Oklahoman stumbled to the ground. Terry followed him and reapplied the guillotine. This time he had his long legs in position to provide leverage. I sprang out of my seat. It was in deep. Grice struggled but he was snared.

A choke is as thrilling as it gets. With a knock out, you know very little about it. You leave a hole in your defence, you're tagged- goodnight. With a choke, there's the set up, the application, then the eventual realisation that there is no way out. At that point, there is a choice to make. Tap to submit or keep on resisting in the vain hope of escape. Grice dug in. Staring at the big screen, we all shared the moment. In the small slit under the American's eye curtain, the intense pupils were replaced by rolling white emptiness. The ref dived in to stop it. As the choke was released, Grice's limp body slumped to the canvas. The loser was surrounded by medics. The winner mounted the fence and milked the roars of the crowd. I'd got totally caught up in the action and cheered along with the rest. Each replay looked sweeter than the last. An epic debut performance from Etim.

A wave of communal goodwill washed over the cheap seats. Strangers exchanged nods and smiles as they hailed the victor. The love was spreading, but had it had bypassed the person in the seat next to mine

- I want to go out the back.

To say that Lucy had not bought into the fight as much as I had would be an understatement. The effects of the afternoon ale and ten minutes in the heat rich/oxygen poor environment of block 217 had taken their toll.

Often, you read about big events in the paper and

there's a little paragraph about people collapsing due to the heat/excitement. I always assumed that this was just a way for journalists to fill a column. Any people who were a bit pissed or had a sit down through being tired were lumped together as overcome by heat or emotion in a bid to sensationalise a story. Surely people don't really just flake out- do they?

We'd managed three steps when it happened. Lucy stopped. Her legs buckled and she went down on her arse. She wasn't out, but she was in no state to continue. In the style of a Victorian lady, it had all become too much for her.

After she'd spent a minute on a spare aisle seat, I went off to get her a drink of water. I returned after a couple of minutes with a plastic glassful. By this time, she was receiving expert medical attention. Some tached up bloke was offering her a pint of bitter.

- Get that down you luv and you'll feel fine.

In times of crisis- the true Brit spirit shines through.

Later, Lucy told me that, for five minutes, she couldn't understand anything that was being said and everything happened in slow motion and in black and white. I was going to tell her that it reminded me of a day out in Blackburn but I thought it might sound like I was making light of her traumatic experience.

We went out the back and dodged a steward to head right down to the emergency exit doors to suck some fresh air in. Lucy confided that, at first, she thought that

BLOODY REVOLUTION

Etim had strangled Grice. She couldn't understand why he was celebrating and everyone was cheering when Matt Grice had just been murdered.

I suppose that for a first timer seeing someone getting choked out is weird. Unlike a punch, any choking in a film results in death. Seeing someone being choked out, in close up on a 30 foot screen you can nearly touch, is pretty intense. Factor in the gas mark seven temperature and the shortage of oxygen and it's enough to make anyone swoon.

I had a dilemma; on the one hand, my relationship with Lucy. She had recovered, but passing out is definitely going to put a bit of a downer on your evening. Once you get used to it- it's a doddle. Jiu jitsu guys go on about the joys of oxygen deprivation so much, I'm sure most of them spend their leisure time involved in Michael Hutchence style activities. When you're a first time fainter, I reckon you're going to feel a bit delicate. Surely I had to do the right thing and take her home. No way was she going to enjoy the rest of the night after this. It's was my duty to do the right thing.

On the other hand- IT'S THE UFC BABY.

I realised I had to come up with a compromise that satisfied all parties. Lucy was putting a brave face on it, saying she'd be happy to stick it out while looking like she relished the prospect as much as she would a hot date with John McCririck. I met her halfway by pitching the idea that we would leave before the main event so we could miss the traffic. Mirko 'Cro-Cop' Filopovic had come over from the Japanese promotion Pride and was being fast tracked to a shot at the Heavyweight title. In Manchester, he was matched against Gabriel Gonzaga. In my eyes, this was as close to a gimme as you would ever get in the UFC. Cro-Cop would be able to keep the stocky grappler at distance and pick him off. Like I told Lucy; it'll be a first round head kick knockout. It was no sacrifice as I was off to a Muay Thai show the next day so I'd be seeing plenty of that kind of biz. Plus I wasn't mad about the idea of spending two hours getting out of the car park myself.

We went back in and took our seats ready for the main card. Lucy was too busy concentrating on remaining conscious to chat and the old blokes next to us were taking pedantic arguments about which is the best martial art to new depths of dullness. And did I forget to mention- it was hot. I was seriously ready to pitch the idea of us beating the car park rush by three hours and fucking the whole thing off as a bad job.

Right then, I spied a steward going round having furtive chats with couples who would then slide away. There was always a chance they were being lured into some depraved white slavery/snuff movie type deal but anything was preferable to staying put in block 217. I went over and asked the bloke what the crack was. He told me he had some seats to fill downstairs, but he only had one pair left. Rising above the fact he thought I was in some way associated with the pricks I'd been sat next to, I asked him how much this was going to set me back. 'Nothing' he said. Sold.

Whether it was company policy, a ploy to fill up visible seats for TV or just a guy doing random good deeds...frankly, who cares? We were off to the land of milk and honey. Downstairs, row T. In the thick of it, not watching from above. Luxurious seats firmly in the three figure price bracket. And you could breathe. You could breathe real, almost fresh, barely recycled air. Our time on the dark side made us all the more grateful and, as you are well aware, free stuff always tastes better.

The lights dimmed and the expectation levels rose. With a fanfare, the screens confirmed that it was time for the real main event. It wasn't billed as such but, for everyone bar the Croatian contingent and the anoraks, UFC 70 was all about Michael Bisping. The Lancastrian was a key figure in the Battle for Britain. He was fresh from winning the third season of the UFC's reality show The Ultimate Fighter. The show was screened on Bravo, giving 'The Count' a Dog the Bounty Hunter level of fame. In his role as the UK poster boy, Bisping had been doing an endless round of interviews, fielding moronic questions about the movie Fight Club and whether he was a barbarian who battered people in the street. Thankfully, the time for talking was over.

His opponent, the Aussie Elvis Sinosic, entered to a reasonable amount of abuse. Bisping was a heavy favourite, but I wasn't so sure. I'd interviewed Elvis at the weigh in the day before and he was all business. His best days were behind him, but there was plenty of fight left in the 'King of Rock and Rumble'.

Bisping returned as the conquering hero, clad in a brown hoodie and camouflage board shorts. He sprinted through the arena like a man possessed. Always a bad sign. He seemed too keyed up; too eager to please the expectant horde. I was wrong. The first round went to plan. The Brit took his man down and let him have it on the ground; a continuous barrage that left Elvis with a bad cut on his forehead.

Sinosic came out for the second looking a mess; his dyed silver hair contaminated with dirty blood. The head trauma made him forget his lines. He dropped the star of the show with a knee and went close with first an elbow lock then a choke attempt. The M.E.N. held its breath. Bisping escaped, the M.E.N. roared like Ricky Hatton was back in the house. With Elvis on his back, Bisping let him have it. The fight was stopped. The roof came off. Bisping's flirtation with defeat had made victory taste so much sweeter. I looked around at the reaction and drank it in. Pure, unadulterated joy. Next to me, Lucy was applauding and cheering. MMA really was going to kick off big time in the UK. Us believers had been right all along.

As soon as we got home, I fired up the computer. After a couple of minutes, I found a video of the main event. As everyone had predicted, it was a first round headkick KO.

BLOODY REVOLUTION

As almost nobody had predicted, it was Gonzaga who had knocked out the highly touted specialist kickboxer.

How can you not love this sport?

PEACE IN OUR TIME

British Fighting Championship Draw
Ultimate Training Centre, Birmingham
13th February 2009

Friday the thirteenth. Not an ideal choice for a new beginning but at least the venue was a step up in class. For years, UK fighters had toiled away in back street dumps or long lost corners of draughty leisure centres. Coming into the U.T.C. some of them were open mouthed; like Latin American peasants who'd just stormed the presidential palace and couldn't quite take in the riches in front of them. A competition ready cage, full size boxing ring, pristine matted wrestling area, free weights, cardio machines; all branded and housed in a shiny steel and glass package. The showers even had hot water for crying out loud.

The fighters had tagged along with a bunch of people you could describe as the movers and shakers of the UK

MMA scene. Usually, when you get a group of rival promoters in the same room, the tension is so thick you expect Gazza to stroll in with a chicken dinner and a fishing rod. Today was a different story. Relations were cordial verging on downright jolly. After years of internecine warfare, they were finally going to give peace a chance.

When talking about the UK MMA scene, there are no hard facts. Who was first? Who put on the best shows? Who did the most to push the sport forward? The answer to these questions depends on who you are talking to at the time. There is no definitive history, just mythology and hearsay. One article of faith unites all those involved: MMA is the fastest growing sport in the world and will eventually become massive in Britain. This mantra has attracted devout martial arts evangelists, chancers hoping to cash in and plenty of people who have a foot in both camps. To date, none of them has managed to make the prophecy a reality.

Represented at the U.T.C. were Ultimate Warrior Challenge (Southend), FX3 (Reading), AMMA (West Midlands), Paul Murphy (formerly of the Doncaster based Ultimate Force) and Cage Warriors (Midlands). These were all promotions that had a reputation for doing things the right way. The little things; like proper weigh ins, fair matchmaking and paying what they'd agreed. While these might seem like minimum requirements to an outsider, they were not guaranteed in the Wild West world of UK MMA.

The thing that separates MMA from virtually every other sport in the UK is the lack of governing body. In the United States, the UFC and other MMA organisations come under the control of the various state athletic commissions. Fighters have to undergo drug testing and medical suspensions can be imposed when necessary. From start to finish, the athletic commission holds the whip hand and can pull the plug on anything they deem unacceptable. In the UK, all regulation is voluntary and, from the banking crash to Sonia off Eastenders' yo-yo dieting, we all know how successful self regulation is.

Unregulated should not be confused with illegal. Unlicensed boxing thrives away from the British Boxing of Control (BBoC) and, in football, anyone can have a kick about without registering with the FA. No regulation has plus points. For a start, promoters don't have to fork out thousands for a license...and that's about it. The downside is massive. Unlike boxers, MMA fighters are not required to take a medical before they begin their careers. If they get knocked out or injured, there is no statutory suspension before they can get in the cage again. As with any combat sport, the referee is a crucial actor; both as an adjudicator and a life saver. The mandatory qualifications; being a mate of the promoter. The key ingredient required when putting together a safe, fair and entertaining fight card is good matchmaking. With no official records to go on, promotions have to rely on their own knowledge and any info they can pick up along the way. Some fighters are too keen for their own good, lying about their history to get into fights they aren't ready for. At the other extreme, some fighters will regularly pull out, leaving huge holes on a card. Although they may cite injury as an excuse, often the real reason is a bigger pay day elsewhere.

Without an agency overseeing it, UK MMA operates under the rules of unbridled capitalism- AKA: chaos. As long as you can sell a ticket, you will be forgiven anything. A few promotions have implemented limited testing for performance enhancing drugs. A step in the right direction you might think, but with no official sanctions, how can the results be trusted? If you have Heavyweight doorman who sells 200 tickets to his mates every show, what are you going to do when he tests positive for roids? Send him and his guaranteed £6,000 down the road to your competitor or pour his cup of piss down the bog? With no official rankings or championship structure, why would someone bother to fight away from their own backyard? They will be hit in the pocket and will have to face a hostile crowd (and judges). Local fiefdoms developed as there was no gain for promoters or fighters in looking beyond their own areas. Most shows used the unified (same as the UFC) rules, but were free to tweak them as they pleased.

The British Fighting Championship was going to be the start of a new era. The men behind it had already taken steps to move the sport forward and now they were going to work together to push to the next level. The name British Fighting Championship, or BFC as everyone was already calling it, was a nod to respectability. The organisations represented had names that represented the sensationalist age they were born into. If a poster didn't have words like 'warrior' and 'force' emblazoned on it, it didn't look like a real MMA poster. Smaller shows tended to go for the alliterative alternative: War in Workington, Burnley Brawl, Merthyr Mayhem, Fisting in Fareham (OK, I made the last one up, but you get the picture). The BFC were moving on.

The plan was ambitious: a knockout competition in each of the weight classes from Bantamweight up to Heavyweight. A tubthumping press release promised 12 BFC shows in 2009 including an end of year Night of Champions when the top 2009 season contenders would go head to head for the British belts. A further 6-8 shows were also at the planning stage to cover Northern Ireland, Wales, Scotland, London, the North East and the North West. Total prize money was a cool £250,000 and bullish briefing about TV coverage meant that sponsorship should not be a problem. There would be no more hiding place. Anyone who won their section could justifiably call themselves the best in the country. Reputations would be made and charlatans would be exposed. The joint venture would give fans nationwide the chance to see the best fighting the best. To participate, you had to submit to the rulings of the BFC. Cards were being kept close to the chest, but this seemed like the emergence of a de facto governing body. If you wanted to share the jam, you had to sign up for the whole shebang.

The draw began. UFC fighters Dan Hardy and Paul Taylor took turns drawing the numbered balls from an orange bucket. The eventual tournament winners would surely be the next batch of Brits to follow them to the big show. On the mic, a suited and booted Jeremy 'Bad Boy' Bailey called the names of the fighters. Bailey had been a face on the scene since as far back as the Millennium Brawl in 1999. His profile had remained high despite a run of poor results thanks to his larger than life personality and ability to sell a fight. These gifts made his switch to promoting an obvious move.

As the names were called, there were a few playground gasps from the throng. The biggest reactions came when some of the old stagers drew each other. In the Lightweight bracket, Paul 'Hands of Stone' Jenkins was paired with Sami 'The Hun' Berik. In his 100 plus fights, 'The Hands' had fought everybody who was anybody. Sami, with his weird kung fu stylings, had a similar disregard for dodging live opponents. Basically, if you've ever been to a UK MMA event in your life, the chances are you'll have seen one or both of them fight. Mark Weir drew Alex Reid in the Middleweights. Universal intake of breath.

Both had been written off as done by many people in the game, but a fight between the pair had huge appeal. The first round of their fight five years earlier, on the old skool Extreme Brawl show, had been a classic of its kind. Two flesh rock em sock em robots punching the hell out of each other for five minutes. The rematch would give one of them a much needed win. The draw went on and on until all the brackets were filled. The lighter weight classes were stacked with talent, but the bigger categories had not attracted as much interest. Heavyweight and Light heavyweight failed to attract enough entrants of a reasonable standard to fill out a full 16 man bracket. With so many tasty match ups to drool over, this was hardly noticed.

While the post draw press conference was being set up, a few fighters came over to me and asked for a bit of intel on the guys they'd been matched with. It always amazes me how little some fighters follow the sport. Even in this YouTube age, it's not uncommon on fight day for someone to approach me and ask if the bloke he's getting into the cage with an hour later likes to stand up or take it to the ground. At the U.T.C., each fighter who got the lowdown from me reacted by nodding and commenting how it was a perfect match up for them. The standard fighter's response: never publicly acknowledge the possibility of defeat.

The top table was ready for questions. Scanning the line up, the absentees stood out. The North East is MMA mad, yet there was no representative from either Strike 'n' Submit or Total Combat. I was trying work out if there was any beef between them and the players present, but I could only come up with images of them smiling and complimenting each other. Perhaps a bigger deal was the absence of the Cage Gladiators crew. Chris Zorba and Emile Coleman ran top quality events at the Liverpool Olympia. Their shows were always stacked with talent from the Wolfslair and Kaobon gyms and were undoubtedly up there with the best in the UK. The success of the Scousers had been rewarded with a TV deal; a highlights package from Cage Gladiators shows was being aired on late night ITV 4. No doubt, they were on the up. I didn't know if it was hubris or contractual detail that had kept them away. Whatever the reason, they were missed.

The biggest problem- there was no Dave. Even if you are only a nodding acquaintance of UK MMA, you'll know Dave O'Donnell. Bald headed, shouty, Cockney geezer. Used to put on Cage Rage at Wembley Arena and live on Sky Sports. Built a brand, put on some massive fights and has the hardest working PR lass in the business. He had been burnt when a link up with the American firm ProElite went sour and Cage Rage went down the pan, but he'd bounced back with Ultimate Challenge- selling out venues and back on live TV (Nuts TV). Love him or hate him- you ignore him at your peril. I knew he wouldn't be at the U.T.C. in person, but his presence was hanging over proceedings.

Time for some answers. Go to any MMA press conference and you can guarantee that the opening question will be asked by a keen youngster from a new media outlet 'dedicated to the fastest growing sport in the world'. Most fizzle out in a few weeks when they realise that covering MMA in general and UK MMA in particular is not going to get them a heap of sponsorship. This week's new kids on the block kicked us off by asking the obvious questions.

The season was going to kick off in mid May at the Harvey Hadden Centre in Nottingham. This was a no brainer: the joint had been the venue for Cage Warriors shows for years and they'd built a solid audience. Also in May, the BFC were going to put on shows in Newport and Barnsley. I asked the panel which of the fights they were most looking forward to. Paul James let slip that he'd already signed Reid/Weir for the next FX3 show, but now he'd have to make other arrangements. This was a good sign. People were willing to sacrifice a few quid for the common good. UFC ref and BFC head of rules Marc Goddard also went for Reid v Weir. Plenty of heads nodded. In any scene, there is kudos to be gained from acknowledging the pioneers. Alex Reid was the number 20 UK Middleweight in the latest Cage Gladiators rankings and had not won a fight in four years, but people wanted to believe he had something left.

The elephant in the room was released. Someone asked about a TV deal. All eyes looked to Andy Lillis, Cage

BLOODY REVOLUTION

Warriors head honcho and apparently the Don of the BFC. He savoured the moment then dropped his secret. Highlights of all British Fighting Championship events would be on TV and the Night of Champions would be live. A deal had been done with Bravo.

If he'd announced free beer for life he wouldn't have got a better reaction. For most people, Bravo is the channel that delivers Big Trouble in Thailand and Danny Dyer's Deadliest Men to the nation. For MMA fans, Bravo is the channel that brought their sport to wider attention. Bravo used to show UFC events the day after they happened, earning eternal gratitude from the hordes that used to have to rely on traded VHS tapes to keep up to date. The BFC were going to get the same exposure. New fans and new money were going to flock to the sport. The good times were going to roll.

I caught up with a few faces for interviews afterwards. Everyone was riding the wave of positivity. Ian Butlin (coincidentally a subject of a Danny Dyer's Deadliest Men) was eager for the challenge after a difficult year.

- I've had a few problems in my personal life, some of them my own fault. I've been stabbed twice and I've been shot.

One of the best things about the sport was the way fighters would always be completely candid. I hoped that, even though UK MMA was now about to gatecrash the mainstream, the open access policy and honesty would remain.

The last person I grabbed a word with was Ian 'Kainer' Dean: the Cage Warriors matchmaker. Kainer is well known for his unrelenting pessimism- an occupational hazard for anyone who lives the UK scene 24/7. His disposition is not helped by the litres of Red Bull he guzzles every day. I was expecting nervous hope, tempered with fears of sabotage and backstabbing. Instead, I got unbridled optimism.

- It's gone amazingly well. I never believed that, in the UK MMA scene, people could work together like this. I think it's a real landmark.

You wouldn't find a dissenting voice in the room. This was history in the making...or so we thought.

On April 25th 2009, Dan Korbely defeated James Saville on an AMMA card to qualify for the first round proper of the Bantamweight tournament. It was the first British Fighting Championship fight. It was also the last.

The collapse of the BFC is another mythical episode in the history of UK MMA. There were a few pull outs, but that goes with the territory. After a great deal of investment, the TV deal went west, taking the sponsors with it. Allegations of sabotage flew around for a while, but nothing criminal. The TV business can give the fight game a run for its money when it comes to sharp practice. The BFC soldiered on for a few days, but Lee Whitehead of MMAWeekly broke the story of their demise early in May. In June, Bravo televised the first show by the British

Association of Mixed Martial Arts (BAMMA). BAMMA's bosses were primarily TV people and they relied heavily on the industry knowledge of one Dave O'Donnell. They stated their intention: to put on tournaments to determine the best fighter in each weight class. By the end of July, O'Donnell had left, slagging the BAMMA brass in the media.

The British Fighting Championship was dead and the idea of co-operation and conciliation between promoters died with it.

STYLE VERSUS STYLE

10th Legion Championship Fighting
Gemtech Arena, Hull
27th September 2009

Marcus Da Silva strolls to the cage- a picture of concentration. In the stands, his students are raising the roof, but he blocks it all out and focuses on the job in hand. He is wearing a traditional martial arts kimono, secured by a brown belt. When he reaches the cage door, he takes care to neatly fold the belt and hand it to his cornerman before entering.

His opponent is keeping loose and doing his best to look unimpressed. Minutes earlier, Lanus Jones had performed a standard ring walk; swaggering along to the Kaiser Chiefs' 'I Predict a Riot'. Lanny's fight wear was a clue to his style of fighting; TapouT board shorts in the colours of the Mexican flag. In boxing, from Ricky 'The Manchester Mexican' Hatton to Michael Gomez, all action, never say die punchers have venerated the no backward step philosophy of fighters from south of the border. Jones was more than a slugger. Like the other Manvers lads, he had better wrestling than most UK operators and his submission game was coming along. He had played it down when I talked to him earlier; describing his jiu jitsu level as 'lower than white belt'.

The two are called together in centre cage by the referee for their final instructions. The shape of the forth-coming fight was obvious. Da Silva is a Brazilian jiu jitsu specialist. At the inaugural 10th Legion show, he had wrapped his legs round Jaime Palou, transitioned to an armbar and hung on for dear life. The Swede Palou struggled manfully to shake Marcus off, but finally had to surrender. That effort earned Marcus the 10th Legion Championship Fighting Light heavyweight belt. Lanus was here to take it off him. This was a genuine throwback fight. Style versus style. Brazilian jiu jitsu versus the world.

Brazilian jiu jitsu was developed by the Gracie family. Without the Gracies, there would be no UFC, no MMA, no insightful magazine articles by yours truly. They revolu-tionised the way we think about fighting. The weird clan of doctor's kids came to the conclusion that, eventually, every fight ends up on the floor. Building on their judo foundations, they devised the ultimate ground fighting system. The key player was Helio, the runt of the litter. He perfected a set of chokes and joint manipulations that enabled a small weak guy to beat a larger adversary. Brains beats brawn. The wee Helio achieved celebrity status in Brazil, taking on all comers. He threw out a challenge to Heavyweight boxing champ Joe Louis: a no rules fight, one million dollars, winner takes all. The Brown Bomber never got back to him. Along with the invention of killer submissions from the bottom, the Gracie's came up with an all encompassing philosophy of combat and a banana heavy diet plan. Of the next generation, it was Rorian who took the family art to the next level. The law graduate moved to California in 1979. He had grand plans of spreading the word, but wound up working as an extra on Starsky and Hutch, co-ordinating fights for movies and teaching jiu jitsu in his garage. He came to prominence thanks to an article in Playboy magazine in September 1989 entitled; 'Rorion Gracie is willing to fight to the death to prove he's the toughest man in the west'. The piece outlined the story of his extraordinary family and contained details of the marketing ploy known as the Gracie challenge: Rorion would fight anyone-$100,000, winner takes all.

Art Davie was an advertising man with an eye for an opportunity. He signed up for private tuition at Gracie's gym. As Davie discovered more about jiu jitsu, he saw the chance to use his creative nous. Together with Rorian, he put together the idea of a one night tournament that pitted martial artists of different styles against each other. The pair sold the idea to the Semaphore Entertainment Group; a firm with a reputation for offbeat pay per view TV events.

The Ultimate Fighting Championship was staged at the McNichols Sports Arena in Denver (Colorado had no boxing commission to press them on inconvenient matters like safety). Eight fighters of various levels of distinction were assembled: a couple of kickboxers, a couple of guys with karate credentials, a sumo wrestler, a boxer, a shoot wrestler and a Gracie. Rorion selected his brother Royce. Royce was young, clean cut and slender compared to the grizzled hulks in the other corner. In the quarter final he faced the boxer Art Jimmerson, who gave up when Royce mounted him on the canvas. In the semi and final, he took down his opponents and choked them into submission.

The show did reasonable numbers and, as is the way in the entertainment business, a sequel was planned. Once again, Royce Gracie brushed aside the opposition to take the title. Over time, what we now know as the modern sport of Mixed Martial Arts evolved from these humble beginnings. If anyone other than Royce had triumphed, this would not have happened. Viewers were entranced by the antics of this skinny kid. The notions of what is effective in martial arts changed overnight. It became accepted that, in a one on one fight, a grappler will beat a striker.

There is scientific evidence to back up this assertion. Shortly after the first UFC, the US Army began a root and branch overhaul of their hand to hand combat training under the supervision of Matt Larsen. The staff sergeant managed the kind of experiments you can only run when you are a fighting force with hundreds of thousands of recruits every year. Take a class of 100 infantrymen and split them into two groups. Fifty of them learn boxing from pro coaches for twenty hours as part of their induction, the other fifty do additional physical training. In the final week of training, the two groups meet in the ring. The non boxers will win more than the boxers. Repeat the experiment with ground grappling instead of boxing and the grapplers achieve close to a 100% success rate. The resulting Modern Army Combatives Program is based on what Larsen calls the 'rice and beans' fight plan: 'close the distance, achieve the dominant body position, finish the fight'.

A spectacle designed to take an extra couple of bucks out of the wallets of cable viewers had created a phenomenon. If you wanted to be taken seriously as a martial artist, you had to get a ground game. Gracie jiu jitsu was a hot property. It delivered what every fighting system had always promised. You could defeat any opponent with technique, regardless of his size. Royce Gracie's giant slaying exploits were proof.

BLOODY REVOLUTION

The Gracie family were the vanguard, but ever since, a steady stream of South Americans have left their homeland to satisfy the global demand for authentic BJJ instruction. One of them ended up in Hull.

Marc Goddard is laying down the law. The ref has had enough of Lanus Jones holding the cage. A couple of times, Da Silva has had him in his grasp and Lanny has grabbed the fence to keep on his feet. He knows that the fight is over for him if he gets dragged to the floor; the natural habitat of the Brazilian. Goddard parades the Yorkshireman, instructing each judge to take a point from him. The ref then theatrically crosses his open palms then parts them to let everyone know the score. Jones does it again and he's out of there. The fight recommences. Jones loads up on a right hand, looking for the finish. Marcus traps him against the barrier, tying him up. The chants of 'Lanny, Lanny' ring out from the fans that have made the trip up the M18. Suddenly, Da Silva unloads a couple of uppercuts. Jones manages to break free. The pair exchange punches. For a second, it looks like Da Silva's lost the playbook and is going to trade. Then, the inevitable happens. They're in centre cage. Marcus puts his arms around his opponent's neck, leaps to hook his feet together round the back and drops backwards. No cage to grab and no back up plan. They fall together.

For the first time, the BJJ students make a noise. There can only be one outcome. As Renzo, the most amiable

Gracie, famously said: 'A boxer is like a lion, the greatest predator on land, but you throw him in the shark tank and he's just another meal.' The arm is in and the legs are creeping up the back for a triangle choke. He's not quite got it and attempts the transition to an armbar. Too late. In a split second, Jones gets the soles of his feet on the deck and powers up and out. He stands over Da Silva and waves him up. As soon as the Brazilian is back on his feet, Lanus confidently marches towards him. He's out of the mole hole and ready to enjoy the sunshine. Da Silva clinches up again but the rejuvenated Jones is having none of it and uses his strength to push him away. As they part, Lanny's right hand pushes the Da Silva right hand down, leaving him exposed. The chin is up in the air, crying out for a fist. Jones obliges, swinging the big left hand in. Timber! The ref is straight on the scene. One punch on the canvas and it's waved off. Lanny does an impromptu lap of honour and the South Yorkshire fans erupt.

There used to be the old saying that records were for DJs, but having that 0 intact is a powerful marketing tool, especially when you're knocking over decent quality. This win means Lanny retains his perfect record and the buzz is building. I caught a word with the victor before I got off. He was full of bravado.

- All this jiu jitsu. Load of bollocks. Just give 'em a good thump. Job done.

BLOODY REVOLUTION

If Lanus Jones had fought on the original UFC show, there would not have been a UFC 2.

WOMEN

A shot rang out.

- AAAARRRGH

The scream was sickening. A high pitched mixture of extreme pain and horror. As one, the crowd in the Gemtech Arena sprang to their feet; their eyes drawn to the shriek, their heads telling them they aren't going to like what they see.

The sound subsides to a near sob. The ring card girl is in her early twenties and wearing the standard gear: blonde extensions, crop top and shiny black hot pants. At a nearby table, a bloke in his best shirt has a bottle in his hand. His face is a study in shock. His eyes flit around for support and betray a sparkle of hope. Everyone's going to see the funny side. Right? The girl rubs furiously at her thigh, just below her spandex panty line. Suddenly, she realises that she is the centre of attention. She holds up her hand and shows her palms in explanation- a mess of mud and recently sprayed champagne. One last indignant volley:

- My fake tan. Ruined!

Sex and violence. Violence and sex. Two inextricably linked words. Seems you can't have one without the other. The fight game is not the only sporting arena that spices up proceedings with fem flesh, but it is the most blatant example. Formula 1 circuits are knee deep in promotional totty, but you don't get lasses straddling the cars and jiggling their tits during pit stops.

Like announcers in shiny suits and awful judging, MMA nicked the idea from boxing. Ring card girls are a relatively late invention. In the old days of pugilism, it was often a little kid who would do a lap to inform the plebs in the cheap seats what round was coming up. Now, it seems that no fight night is too lowly to hire some scantily clad lovelies to impart this vital information. The public demand glamour.

Ring girls have always been something I've had a problem with in MMA. Most fights are three rounds. Surely the most mentally challenged fan can keep track without assistance. Once a promoter accepts he is going to pander to the base elements of the crowd the only question is: how low will he go? Some get bashful and aim for the classy approach with a lass in an evening frock. As my old granddad used to say: you can put a raincoat on a talking parrot but he'll never be Columbo. If a lass is there purely to be ogled, her attire is irrelevant.

Most shows opt for either local lasses or bought in lapdancers. Those who go for the former get nervous smiles, flabbier midriffs and the whiff of Dutch courage. The majority go pro- showcasing harder bodies and dead eyes behind gleaming teeth. Lapdancing clubs continue to multiply despite the fact that, in any major town or city, it is possible to buy full sex in a sauna than it is to have a private dance. The ultimate triumph of style over substance. Men paying to feel more frustrated.

The lovely girls are called upon to provide photo dress-ing, adorn the cage and add allure to ring walks. Even this is not enough for some. Total Combat in Sunderland is as respectable as it gets in terms of the fights, offering opportunities to the mushrooming ranks of novices. For some inexplicable reason, they have steep ramp leading down from the changing room area. The fighters, in trainers, literally take this in their stride. For a ring girl in stilettos, it is reminiscent of an episode of Total Wipe-out. Each entrance sees the lass shorten her step, take a deep breath then dash down at pace, hoping to avoid a spill. At best, this is the invention of an evil genius obsessed with making bosoms bounce. The alternative explanation is a misogynistic plot aimed at destroying beauty by way of horrific carpet crashes.

BLOODY REVOLUTION

Of course, any talk of ring girls must include a mention of Cage Rage. Their Wembley extravaganzas were as much about exotic dancing as they were about fighting. The evening would start with a cage full of gyrating crotches and a glitter cannon (for the uninitiated, that really was a cannon that fired glitter). Breaks between rounds would get the stripper army up off their stools to shake their thang on the runway. At cageside, promo lasses would wobble their tits for any camera and generally act cheap on demand. The reaction of the fans away from the hall was instructive. The Cage Rage girls were always out in the foyers, mingling and flirting unconvincingly. When posing for photos with them, the punters would put their arms round them and do the classic fighter pose- clenched fist aimed at the chin. Force of habit or an unconscious reaction to how the women were being presented?

How are the audience supposed to react? I was at a show in the Midlands a few years ago. There was only one girl on duty. The first time she did a lap with the round card, a guy in the crowd shouted out. I couldn't see him, just heard his booming voice like everyone else.

- Get your tits out.

This got a huge laugh. I laughed. It was so over the top. He was obviously taking the piss. End of round one.

- Get your tits out.

Laughter. End of round two

- Get you tits out.

42

Laughter. And so it went on. And on. And on. Sometimes he'd wait till she was almost getting out to shout the order for maximum impact, but most of the time it'd be an exact repeat. The laughs kept coming. Nasty laughs. Conspiratorial Bernard Manning laughs. This wasn't some Sid the Sexist satire. It's an obvious progression. The ring card girl is a ridiculous figure. The natural reaction must be to treat her with contempt and ridicule her. The guy may have been disrespectful, but how can you slag him off. If you present a person merely as an object, you can't expect others to treat them with any respect.

The ubiquity of ring girls ignores the make up of the typical UK MMA crowd. Events pull a far bigger female audience than most sports and this is only half the story. Live MMA attracts a large amount of good looking women dressed to impress. While male spectators adhere to a casual dress code, a sizeable chunk of the lasses turn up resplendent in high heels and low cut dresses with high hemlines. Once again, the sickly smell of sex hangs in the air.

It is in no way patronising to suggest that some of the women who watch MMA in the flesh are as interested in the flesh as the MMA. Let's not pretend this doesn't happen the other way either. I've spent many hours in front of the telly entranced by the early, uneven rounds of the women's 110 metre hurdles. There used to be cracks about women who watch football only going to look at the men's legs. The fact is, the likes of Cristiano Ronaldo don't look like men. They look like moisturised boyband rejects. Footballers don't act like men anymore either. Didier Drogba is a huge battering ram of a chap, yet he spends most of his time sulking like a three year old girl. The culture of the game encourages infantile behaviour. Players are rewarded for diving and holding their heads after being grazed on the shin. It's hardly surprising that real women are looking elsewhere for stimulation.

Our idea of sport is heavily based on the Ancient Greek Olympics. Their events have survived, unlike the Romans, whose Christian slaughtering and bear related high jinks have no place in our health and safety loving age. When all the running and throwing stuff was over, the real sport would begin. The climax of the games was all about fighting: boxing, wrestling and pankration (basically MMA). The participants would all perform stark bullock naked. Married women were not allowed to attend, but young single women were. Some historians suggest that maidens were actively encouraged to turn up by their families in the hope that they could pull one of the athletes. For the duration of the games, prostitutes from all around headed into town to service the testosterone high spectators.

In other gatherings across every continent of the world there is evidence of fights being staged at harvest celebrations with the prettiest bride in the village as a prize. Fertility, fighting, sex- as old as the hills.

One group who do not fit into the sex/violence continuum are female fighters. From rough and tumbling little boys to world leaders at the summit table, males will measure their worth based on their ability to compete physically against their peers. An unofficial ranking system develops with the big hitter at the top. It's the masculine way. The whole capitalist system is an extension of this dog eat dog mindset with the victors erecting huge phallic monuments to their dominance. Women are not judged in the same way. The ability to beat others down is not a cherished feminine quality.

In the modern era, organised female fighting falls into two distinct camps: martial arts and prizefighting. The traditional martial arts have always valued women. As self defence systems, they are suitable for both genders. Women compete at Olympic level in judo and tae kwon do and clubs welcome girls. Female prizefighting is another story altogether. Professional women's boxing is a sick joke. The standard has oscillated between poor and unacceptable and the integrity of the sport is questionable. Lookers with a back story build padded records that even embarrass boxing devotees (a tough task). When a female bout is featured on a regular bill, it is little more than a freak show to be gawped at. The man in the street appears to have no stomach for seeing women fight with each other. No demand means no money means no future.

Women's MMA, or as some tiresome people call it FeM-MA, falls between the two stools. Gina Carano is the world's most famous female fighter and her career is a lesson in how female MMA is presented. Gina is a good fighter. Gina is also, by common consent, a hot chick. She clocked up a decent Muay Thai record, but achieved fame from her stint as Crush in the TV series American Gladiators. Her early ventures into MMA were successful, but she developed a reputation for having a cavalier attitude to making weight. Promoters keen to keep onside with the golden girl bent over backwards to accommodate her. In 2007, she began fighting for ProElite under their EliteXC banner. The firm was managed by boxing guys and followed boxing principles- build stars to hook the punters. They bet the farm on Kimbo Slice, a bearded heavyweight who had made his name from YouTube videos of him fighting bareknuckle at Florida barbecues, and Carano. A new weight class of 140 lbs was set up- presumably to suit their female star. Forums were split on Carano. Half felt her easy ride devalued MMA. Half wrote indecent dissertations about what position they'd like to get her trapped in.

Gina Carano was one of the hottest properties in MMA and was instrumental in getting EliteXC a network TV deal. The roof fell in when Kimbo was KOd in eight seconds flat by undercard Light heavyweight Seth Petruzelli live on CBS. His employers also bit the dust. Gina crawled from the wreckage with her fame intact, but the public were not in the mood to be cheated anymore. In her next fight, she would have to fight someone who was both a decent fighter and the same size as her. Strikeforce snapped up Gina and matched her against Cristiane 'Cyborg' Santos. For the first time a female bout headlined a major televised card. The pretty girl got beat in the first round and the chance of another female bout headlining a major televised card nosedived.

An early Carano victim was the UK's number one female fighter, Rosi Sexton. Gina came out on top courtesy of some interesting refereeing and a huge weight advantage. As well as being the top woman, Rosi is the third most famous cage fighter in Britain (data source-the author's opinion) thanks to the plethora of newspaper features about her background and choice of profession. Once upon a time, I was helping out a writer who was developing a TV drama about female fighters. I told her about Rosi: First in Maths at Cambridge, PhD in Theoretical Computer Science, accomplished pianist, qualified osteopath and once almost tore a girls foot off her leg in a fight in Costa Rica. The screen writer told me that the audience would never buy it- a case of the truth being stranger than fiction. Rosi outgrew the domestic scene and has travelled the globe to find suitable opponents.

The most widely seen female fight in the UK did not involve Rosi. It took place at Cage Rage 25 in March 2008. Live on Sky Sports, Aisling Daly took on Aysen Berik. Ais the Bash came in with some solid names on her unbeaten record. Aysen was making her debut. She described herself as a stand up fighter, but all her appearances on promo videos suggested she was a total novice who had not yet learnt how to throw a punch properly. On the plus side, she was very pretty.

Aysen wore a tight black rashguard. Draped on the cage fence in the announcements were the usual Cage Rage dollies in their black and pink bras and pants.

The fight went exactly as you'd expect. Berik was game as you like and hung in as long as she could, but she was overwhelmed and beaten up on the deck until her brother Sami waved the white towel of surrender. Aisling danced round in delight. Sami tenderly reassured his defeated sister.

Away from this human drama, the tacky trappings were unchanged. Black and pink bra girls entered the cage to hang off the fence. Black and pink bra girls thrusted their hips on the runway. After the official decision, black and pink bra girls were offered up to the winner to present the trophy. They giggled and kissed the air from a safe distance. The whole thing had been uncomfortable from start to finish. An awful mismatch dressed up as a competitive contest. Two women giving their all amid a sea of women acting like cut outs from porn mags. A novelty act stuffed between the real action.

Female MMA struggles on in this country. There is no obvious route to the big time because there is no big time. For all the conviction that MMA is going to be huge, there is no inkling that female fighters will share the spoils. A large number of women train in the martial arts, but few make the step into the cage. Female fights still make it onto the card of UK shows, but they are invariably low quality affairs. Strangely, for this most macho and unforgiving of sports, no-one seems willing to admit it.

Recently, I was at a UK event that featured a women's fight. As the bout played out, I had a notebook full of negatives: clumsy footwork, no snap, leaves her arm out after a punch, no takedown defence, no attempt to escape. Fair play, the girls were tough and giving it their best, but the skill level was way below all the other fights, including the novices at the start.

During the interval, I was chatting with what passes for the UK MMA press pack. When the subject turned to the female contest, there was a pause. Finally, someone said they'd enjoyed it and everyone agreed- including me I'm ashamed to say. We all filed reports packed with words like 'gutsy', 'plucky' and 'game'. I assumed that everyone had noticed the sloppy technique and naive tactics but had decided to do the gallant thing.

Women's MMA is in danger of being patronised to death. Women's football faces a similar problem. As they are covered on the BBC and get to play in pro stadiums, the England women's team probably think they are genuinely popular and taking part in an exciting sport. The pundits who comment on their matches fuel this sentiment by being overwhelmingly positive. It would be better for everyone if they told the truth. Your sport's a joke: the odd skilful player dominates like a hairy lad in an under 12s game, nobody can head the ball properly and don't even get me started on the goalkeepers. It's great that you're having a go, but don't expect anyone to actually pay proper money to watch this shit.

Women can fight- no question. The women who compete in Olympic sports like judo have a high level of skill and put on fights that are as entertaining as the men's (that is not entertaining- that's why it is subsidised and never on TV). Kickboxing and Thai boxing have been around in the UK for around 35 years. Check out a major card and you will see committed girls in fights that match any male contest in terms of excitement and technical ability. Hopefully, female MMA will reach that level. Until then, it will remain a novelty.

GRAPPLING'S COMING HOME

OMMAC 4,
Liverpool Olympia
6th March 2010

The Olympia: a venue fit for a big fight. Classic interior deco: carved elephants- the lot. Liverpool has always been a fight city. The Scousers don't stick their events out in suburban leisure centres. We're bang on the West Derby Road and the place is buzzing.

Paul Sass was already a star; well a talking point anyway. Nine pro fights, nine pro wins. The extraordinary thing was- the first seven were all by way of triangle choke. His opponents knew what was coming but they couldn't do anything about it. One by one, they stumbled out of the cage- shaking their heads and wearing a 'what happened?' expression. I'd talked to a couple of his victims. Both had been expecting Sass to be all over them like a spider. Instead, he rested back, drew them in and snared them in a split second. A wise old head on young shoulders. Last time out, he'd taken the Olympian Mixed Martial Arts Championships (OMMAC) Lightweight belt from Rob Sinclair in the UK fight of the year. Sass had been pushed to the limit, but hung on to earn a split decision.

Everyone likes to be in the know. Whether it's a four piece beat combo or a fighter, we all want to spot them before they crawl out of the cavern and get noticed. From the boneheads to the orange lasses, the crowd all believe that Sass-mania is about to break out worldwide and they are here to bear witness. The local boy is ready for the big show.

Not long before, I'd interviewed Greg Jackson for a feature. Jackson had built a deserved reputation as the world's premier MMA trainer. Sass had recently spent a few weeks training at his New Mexico gym and the Yoda-like Jackson loudly sang his praises. Despite the expert testimony, I wasn't a true believer. For a start, Sass had never fought away from home. Never mind Liverpool, the lad had not fought anywhere but the cage at the Olympia.

He was not certain to come through the main event anyway. Jason 'Shotgun' Young was no joke. Sass had looked vulnerable in an earlier fight against Jason Ball. Ball was a smart boxer and he'd been the boss standing up. In the final round, one slip in concentration had cost him the fight. Drunk on success, he followed Sass to the mat, and continued the pounding on the floor- looking for the decisive finish. A swivel of the hips and it was all over. Ball was another triangle statistic. Jason Young was a stand up guy. I'd seen him blow a title match at Ultimate Challenge by going to the ground and he wasn't going to make the same mistake twice. In his previous outing, he'd managed to stay standing to get the nod from the judges against Abdul Mohamed- one of the best wrestlers in business. If he could show that level of takedown defence against Sass he'd be in with a great chance. His camp were confident, all Cockney bluster and play fighting.

Cageside, I caught up with the promoter, Chris Zorba. He was always flitting about on fight nights, being more than the perfect host. After he'd made sure my seat was OK and I had a drink, he asked the same question he always did.

- What do you think of the fights?

As usual, there was twinkle in his eye. OMMAC had carried on where the now defunct Cage Gladiators had left off. Their cards always delivered and that night had been no exception. I told him what a great matchmaker he was- the least I could do really.

MMA was booming in the North West and Chris had played a big part in that. Some of the leading camps in the country are based in the Merseyside region and he had provided them with the ideal testing ground. Like every- one, his mind was on the fight at the top of the card. The place was packed and they all wanted to see the local boy.

BLOODY REVOLUTION

The lad who had grown up at the Olympia had come of age. A Liverpool hero. A pure grappler.

The conventional wisdom: the British don't get grappling. Our own martial art, boxing, is in tune with our national character. Straight forward striking. A methodically put together system to deliver the most effective blows possible to knock a man down. None of this kicking- that's simply not British. And none of this wearing pyjamas and spouting philosophical mumbo jumbo. Knock your opponent down, let him up and continue this cycle of blunt force head trauma until he can continue no longer. Sure, the noble art reigned supreme for many years, but deep down, our inner grappler is desperate to resurface.

One day, someone will write a fantastic book about the grappling heritage of Great Britain. If the author is a bold fellow, he will make the case that the United Kingdom is the spiritual home of Mixed Martial Arts. Like the Greeks and societies worldwide, any event with a bit of spare grub and some spare lasses to impress would see British lads stripped down and grappling for dominance. In parts of the nation that are still in touch with the land, like Cornwall and Cumbria, you can see traditional wrestling at country fairs and harvest festivals. Of all the regional styles of wrestling, the one that originated in Lancashire was the most feared. Although it is pretty much unknown in its homeland, catch as catch can or catch wrestling is revered around the globe.

A couple of years ago, I was asked to write a feature piece on catch wrestling by a magazine editor. On the phone, I verbally nodded as he fleshed out the idea despite not really having a Scooby what he was on about. Luckily for me, American catch wrestler Johnny Husky was in the country on a seminar tour so I was able to sign up for a crash course.

Imagine the perfect wrestling coach and you've imagined Johnny Husky: immaculate quiff, patience and a gorgeous Southern drawl. His accent made his constant references to 'riding men hard' particularly hilarious. On a break from the mat, he wised me up:

-Vintage catch wrestling from the Snake Pit gym and all those guys is basically Olympic freestyle style wrestling with submissions. I'm going to get you to the ground and pin you first before I try submissions. We wrestle from position to position. It's the oldest form of wrestling. In catch, if I take him down and an arm's free, that's what I'm grabbing. I will catch you on the fly with a submission whereas Brazilian jiu jitsu wants to work to a position then go for a submission. In other words- I want to constantly be moving. I want to take the shortest route to it rather than setting it up- we call it catching it on the fly. A lot of guys will call it dirty fighting. Carny Style, which is a version of catch as catch can wrestling, is all about me putting elbows on you when I'm riding you. I don't ride you soft. I don't come in and hold you down. I'm either putting a forearm into your throat, a forearm into your rib, radial bone into the arm. It's about me punishing you when you're on the ground. If me and you are on the ground and I'm just holding you, you're going to sit there forever, so I have to give you a shot to make you move, so I can catch that submission. It's rough. You'll have bruises all over you, from elbows, eye sockets, headlocks, it's all about putting the knuckles in and riding hard.

He wasn't kidding. I'd rolled jiu jitsu, but this was something else. All forms of grappling have innate similarities as there are only a certain number of ways you can bend a joint. What grabbed me was the basic nastiness involved. This was jiu jitsu with attitude. Every basic technique came complete with an unpleasant extra to upset your opponent. As with everything down and dirty, there was a tendency to operate below the waist. In jiu jitsu, there is a general reluctance to teach submissions involving leg and heel manipulations to students and heel hooks and knee bars are banned in most competitions for lower graded participants. No such niceties in catch. If it causes pain; grab it and rag it. This isn't a chess game, this is war. Proper fighting. Husky was an enthusiastic teacher, but underneath it all, he harboured a grudge against us Brit's for our carelessness.

- It's a shame that the style started out here and now I have to come over from the US to show it. It's a tragedy.

I'd noticed some disappointment in his eyes when he mentioned the Snake Pit and was greeted with a collective shrug. Other rural forms disappeared when industrialisation triggered the mass migration to the towns and cities. Lancashire wrestling survived and remained a favourite pastime of the industrial working class, particularly the miners. Emigrants spread the word to the US, but the popularity of the pure form of the art began to wane.

- In the old days, the matches lasted too long. You're talking three hour matches, so the fans just bored of it. Then it got onto the carny circuit- which is taking on all comers- a dollar a minute. That got to where people didn't want to get up and fight for a minute. They'd have a stick in the audience. A stick is a ringer you have out in the crowd who'll step up and then you'll put on a pro wrestling show.

A style of fighting that was too tough to live. It transformed into a parody of itself- fake professional wrestling.

A special man kick started the catch wrestling revival in a special town. Wigan is world famous for a number of reasons. Sports fans know it as the home of the greatest rugby league club side in history. Musical and cultural historians know it as the epicentre of Northern Soul, the youth movement that set the blueprint for modern club culture. George Orwell immortalised the town's 'pier' in the title of his investigation into the insidious effects of rampant capitalism on the working class. Sweet toothed, fat bastards revere the birthplace of Uncle Joe's Mint Balls. Everywhere that people take fighting seriously, the names of Billy Riley and the Snake Pit are admired. Everywhere except England.

Billy Riley toured the world taking on all comers. In the 1950s, he returned to Wigan and founded the Snake Pit gym. From this base, he set about reviving the lost art of catch wrestling. Once again, as is often the case with fight stories, we enter the realm of mythology. A few points are generally accepted: the conditions were spartan (showers? the gym didn't even have a bog), Billy Riley was a genius, the training was hard and he produced a crop of exceptional wrestlers. Two of them went on to play massive parts in the development of sport fighting.

Karl Gotch wrestled for Belgium at the 1948 Olympics. A few years later, he was invited up to the Snake Pit and was amazed at the techniques he saw there. He moved to Wigan and lived there for six years as he immersed himself in the scientific art of catch as catch can wrestling. He moved on to the USA where his exploits sparked a resurgence of the forgotten style. Gotch then set up home in Japan where he became known as 'The God Of Pro Wrestling'. The Belgian defeated the local champions and his aggressive style set the example for a new breed of Japanese wrestlers. Native Lancastrian Billy Robinson also ended up in Japan after an illustrious career and set up his own version of the Snake Pit where he taught the wisdom of Wigan to the Tokyo youth. One of his pupils was Kazushi Sakuraba.

Many people rank Sakuraba as the greatest MMA fighter of them all. More importantly, he was the right man in the right place at the right time. When the Pride organization was taking its baby steps, the Japanese public held out little hope of a major home success. The general view was that the local wrestlers would struggle against the much hyped foreign fighters.

By 1999, the Gracie family had an aura of invincibility. To MMA fans, the Brazilian clan were superhumans, always capable of finding a way to win; then along came Sakuraba. First to fall was Royler Gracie at Pride 8. Taking no chances, they sent over undefeated superstar Royce to restore the family honour and demanded special rules including no time limits and taking away the referee's right to stop a contest. Sakuraba's wrestling skills nullified Royce's takedown attempts and his leg kicks began to take their toll. After 90 gruelling minutes, brother Rorian threw in the towel and 'The Gracie Hunter' had claimed another victim. Renzo and Ryan also made the trip to Japan and lost.

Without Sakuraba, Pride would not have flourished as it did. The promotion had a home grown superstar to market. Sakuraba appealed to a wider audience. Brought up in the crazy world of pro-wrestling, he understood how to put on a show. His flamboyant personality and love of masks and capes married to his employer's extravagant production values provided the blueprint for the Oriental MMA spectaculars that changed the face of the sport.

BLOODY REVOLUTION

Sakuraba underlined the fact that jiu jitsu was beatable. In the US, Olympic wrestler Mark Coleman had formulated a plan to posture up and punch when in guard: ground and pound. Now, Sakuraba was beating the first family of jiu jitsu at their own game; by out thinking them and catching them in submissions. Since then, champions like Josh Barnett have demonstrated the effectiveness of catch wrestling at the top level. When man mountain Brock Lesnar switched to MMA, he sought out the tuition of catch guru Erik Paulson. Despite this success, catch is still the black sheep of the grappling family. You can hear the bitterness in Husky's voice:

- Everything is jiu jitsu based now. It's Royce Gracie, it's the UFC. It's what's now. People start on their back. You go to a class and say let's roll and he'll lay down on his back and put his legs up. If me and you are in the street, you don't want to go to your back- so you have to learn how to wrestle.

It makes sense but nobody's listening. The Gracies have a better marketing team. When Brock Lesnar mauled BJJ blackbelt Frank Mir in a UFC title fight, he had him caught up in the classic stockade position. None of the 'experts' on commentary noticed. In contrast, the most obscure jits technique will be identified instantly. Every major town has its own booming, Gracie affiliated school, yet kids in England have never even heard of the style that is part of their heritage.

At the end of the seminar, I shook hands with Johnny Husky and thanked him. Really thanked him. It was the most I'd enjoyed a session at the gym in years. I felt a real connection to catch wrestling. Even the terminology was familiar. In catch, a wrestler who relentlessly batters you on the deck is known as a ripper; someone who uses all the tools at their disposal to cause maximum destruction. My Grandad was a ripper back in the 30s. It was the name given to the miners who worked on the frontline, lying down as they hacked away at the coal face. The dirtiest most dangerous job imaginable. Real tough guys.

The catch moves came so naturally, the philosophy was so refreshingly bullshit free. It all made sense. On the drive home, I started having fanciful thoughts. Maybe I'd got in touch with my ancestors. Catch was the style of my people; the North of England's industrial working class. That's why everything had felt so effortless. It was in me already. Johnny Husky had unlocked my inner Northerner.

The magazine article never got written. I can't remember why. Probably something more important came up. It's catch wrestling you see- nobody's interested.

All night, Brad Pickett has been enjoying the attention. He's up supporting his team mate Jason Young. Pickett had been a face on the UK scene for years; wearing a trilby and playing the Cockney geezer character up to the max at Cage Rage. His ring name is 'One Punch', but his career really took off when he shipped out to American

BLOODY REVOLUTION

Top Team in Coconut Creek, Florida to add wrestling to his game. He'd just clocked up an impressive submission win on his debut for World Extreme Cagefighting, the UFC's sister promotion that showcases the lighter weight classes. Brad didn't need the comic entrances to Chas and Dave tunes to be noticed anymore. Everyone who knew the sport could see he was the real deal. He sensed he was getting envious glances and he loved it.

Not that the Olympia wasn't used to famous guests. The big names from the Wolfslair would always pop down to support their mates: Rampage Jackson, Cheick Kongo and, of course, Michael Bisping. Then there was the other Merseyside powerhouse- Kaobon. Terry Etim may have cracked the UFC, but he was on corner duty at every event, happily carrying the spit bucket for his brothers in arms. Cageside, his fellow UFC Lightweight Paul 'Tellys' Kelly was on hand to roar encouragement. Kelly is the world's most Scouse man. His odd nickname comes from his early days at the Wolfslair, when he supposedly walked round with his chest puffed out so far he looked like he was carrying an invisible TV under either arm. His switch to Kaobon had not dampened his passion and he'd had plenty to shout about already. As usual, the team were piling up the Ws. Submission after submission. Those guys had something other teams didn't; the power of luta livre.

Luta livre (literally free fight) is the black sheep of South American fighting systems. The style emerged from the Brazilian melting pot in the early 20th century and has a lot in common with its proletarian brother catch wrestling. Luta livre came from the streets. Lancashire miners would be kept off their backs by rocks and stones on the ground. Without comfortable mats, there was no place for lying back and playing guard. Later, catch wrestling instructors would stick safety pins into the flesh of their students if they gave up the fight for top position. As in Wigan, the Rio lads knew that getting top control and attacking the knee and ankle joints was the fast track to ending a fight.

Luta livre and Gracie jiu jitsu arrived on the scene at the same time in the same city. Something had to give. For years, a civil war raged. More accurately; a class war. Jiu jitsu was seen as the domain of the middle class, the 'playboy' posers of the Copacabana. Wearing the right gi and being a member of the right club were status symbols. The luta livre massive fought bare chested, like humble grapplers had through the ages. They weren't welcome at the 'right' clubs. Wrong clothes, wrong attitude, wrong address. Resentment, bitterness, hatred- fights. Street showdowns and gym invasions were commonplace as the dispute raged on over the decades until a decisive blow settled matters.

BLOODY REVOLUTION

In 1991, Robson Gracie organized the Grande Desafio (Grand Challenge). The event was a night of fights, each featuring a leading jiu jitsu fighter taking on a luta livre exponent under old skool vale tudo (no holds barred) rules. Brazil's premier TV network Globo screened the event live, thinking they were getting a benign form of boxing without punches that would be suitable for a mainstream audience. Their illusions were shattered as the pure hatred between the warring camps came to the surface in the first fight. Wallid Ismail took Eugenio Tadeu down then repeatedly headbutted him in the face, spreading teeth across the blood soaked canvas. Next up, Murilo Bustamante propelled Marcelo Mendes through the ropes into the baying mob standing at ringside. To complete a 3-0 sweep for jiu jitsu, Fabio Gurgel pounded his way to victory over Denilson Maia. Throughout the event, the atmosphere never dropped below Thunder-dome pitch. The climax sparked a ring invasion, with the triumphant horde bouncing and they chanted 'jiu jitsu'.

Grande Desafio divided the nation. Shocked by the brutality they had witnessed, thousands of older viewers called Globo to protest. Young men flocked to the gym, desperate to emulate the men they had seen on TV. Overnight, participation trebled and jiu jitsu exploded out of Rio to become a nationwide phenomenon. A couple of years later, Royce Gracie infected the rest of the planet with jiu jitsu fever and the rout was complete. If you wanted to make it as a grappler, you signed up for jiu jitsu.

Luta livre disciples will tell you that the real score was 3-2 and they won the rematch but no one is listening. On the basis of a one off TV special- luta livre was consigned to the dustbin of history. The ruling class, with the support of the media, prevail over the poor- it's an old story.

A decade and a half later, MMA is finding its feet in the UK. One team that is gaining respect is Kaobon, supervised by former Thai boxing champ Colin Heron (Kaobon is Thai for heron). Terry Etim and another fighter, Mark Scanlon, head to Brazil to tune up their ground games. In Rio, they meet luta livre blackbelt Marcelo Brigadeiro and forge a bond on the mat. The uncompromising, ungentle art seems a perfect fit for the rigors of modern MMA. They keep in touch and Brigadeiro accepts an invitation to coach in Liverpool in 2008. Ever since, he has been honing the grappling skills of the Kaobon fight team and attracting new converts from across the North of England.

Sass is primed and ready to go. A clean cut, lean everyman with cropped hair and an LFC tattoo on his bicep. A 21 year old with the world at his feet; with everything to lose. No messing, no risks. Immediately, he goes for the takedown. Jason Young strains to keep his feet but Sass topples him. He goes for the triangle; his signature sign off. Young escapes. The crowd gasp. This doesn't happen. Once you're lost in the Sass triangle, there is no return. A push and a pop and Sass has him again. Relief engulfs the spectators. Normal service is resumed. This time it looks tight. Further constriction. Young struggles free again. Unprecedented. Unbelievable. He's got the answer. Sass has been sussed. The one trick pony is off to the glue factory. Sass needs a plan B sharpish. He sees Young's leg undefended. Catch it if you can. Sass grabs the foot. The heel hook is on. Young grimaces. His tendons are ready to snap. There's no way out. He taps.

Sass scales the fence and milks the acclaim. It's mayhem in the stalls. Liverpool, the supreme boxing city, is going crazy for a submission win. A great awakening. A multitude of inner Northerners released. They feel a long forgotten sensation. An echo from the past. A move of the impoverished masses from the battlefield, the village green, the pit head. Incubated in Wigan and Rio. Reborn on Merseyside.

Grappling's coming home.

THE BALLAD OF JIMMY AND JAMES

JIMMY

- I think, psychologically, I've grown in the last year. I've also learnt not to listen to things. I've heard a few things but nothing concrete, no papers or nothing, so in my eyes there's nothing there. I can't see the point in getting frustrated and winding myself up because it's one of them sports where people can change their minds, so I'm just getting on with it. Just keep fighting, keep winning and keep enjoying it.

Jim Wallhead was cool as a cucumber; speaking softly and swirling the ice remnants round the bottom of his glass. Pressure- what pressure? Maybe the fighter doth protest too much.

Jimmy's team mate Dan Hardy was on hand to give his testimony.

BLOODY REVOLUTION

- It's always a weird situation with Rough House. Paul (Daley) was the first one and I was always a bit in his shadow and now, I've moved on and Jimmy was a little in my shadow. It's nice that he's getting the stage he deserves because he is fantastic. To be honest, there isn't anything between me, Paul and Jimmy. We really are quite even in the gym. Jimmy really deserves to fight on a bigger stage and I think that this is a good step up for him before he moves onto the world scene.

Dan had already cracked it. Signed, sealed and delivered. In a month he'd be making his UFC debut. For all its delusions of grandeur, the UK scene is a stepping stone. Hip young gunslingers don't dream about winning a belt at the Rivermead Leisure Centre in Reading. Vegas or Tokyo; that's the end of the rainbow. This was Jimmy's last stop on the road; his last interview full of denial. He'd just weighed in: bang on the money, first time. That's how you do it if you're a serious guy. In a minute, he'd leave the hotel to chow down. A little over 24 hours to kill before the showdown. One more sleep as a pretender. 'Keep fighting, keep winning, keep enjoying it.' Jimmy had been the next big thing right from Jump Street. Now it was time to get paid. To get what he deserved.

Jimmy started out the way loads of lads do. He went to a show with a mate, got caught up in the action and fancied having a go himself. Unlike lots of lads, Jimmy was a judo blackbelt who had represented his country at youth level. He got picked up by the management arm of the Cage Warriors organisation and was invited to train with Team Rough House in Nottingham. Jimmy's stand up improved, making him a true all rounder. The future was bright. 'Keep fighting, keep winning, keep enjoying it.'

In 2006, opportunity knocks. On 48 hours notice, he flies out to the Netherlands to compete in the 2H2H Road to Japan Tournament. The prize- a contract to fight for a major promotion in Japan. Jimmy wins two fights in one night to take the title. The contract offer mysteriously disappears. 'Keep fighting, keep winning, keep enjoying it.'

Next time out, Jimmy beats Jason Tan in front of the hostile Olympia crowd in the Scouser's own backyard. Tan gets signed and his next fight is in the UFC. Jimmy's is in Nottingham against the German Dennis Siver. Siver armbars him in the second and is rewarded with a UFC contract. Jimmy goes on a four fight winning steak, including a one round victory over UFC veteran Steve Lynch. 'Keep fighting, keep winning, keep enjoying it.'

Whispers start going round that BodogFight are about to make an offer, then the promotion ceases trading. A firm contract offer comes in from the International Fight League. The IFL are the new kids on the block, but they've got big ideas and a TV deal in the US. They are going global and they want Jimmy to be the anchorman of their new UK team. The UK team never comes into being and the IFL sinks into a sea of debt. Jimmy drops a decision on the Cage Warriors USA show, but bounces back with a win on home soil. Next up, the experienced Brazilian Fabricio Nascimento in Nottingham.

Enter the Rough House 7 is one of the most impressive cards ever assembled by a domestic promotion. Afterwards, there is only one fight everyone is talking about. Fabricio Nascimento cuts a compelling figure, with the body of an athlete and a hairstyle that looks like a cross between 70s funkateer and a cartoon character who has recently been on fire. Look at the eyes of Nascimento and you see a window into a world of chaos. The Brazilian comes out throwing accurate, single shots and looks to set up a takedown. On the deck- Nascimento goes close with a leg lock attempt, but Jimmy keeps his cool and rolls out of danger. As the round wears on, Jimmy begins to take control of affairs with some slick boxing. Round two and three see the pair trade punches. Once again, Wallhead impresses with his intelligent stand up. Fabricio Nascimento tried to draw his man into a brawl. With each passing second, Fabricio moves further away from sanity. He advances in a stance that resembles a mechanical rooster that is desperate for a piss. He calls Wallhead on-slapping his chest, grinning and keeping up a demented commentary. Judo Jim responds with sharp blows, but keeps his work organised and avoids taking unnecessary risks.

The crowd go crazy throughout and give the local boy a huge ovation when he takes a unanimous decision. It's beyond a fight. It's an event. The kind of experience you can't get anywhere else. Drama, comedy, pain suffering, ecstasy- all played out for real. A bravura performance from a man at the top of his game.

So here we are. Back at the Harvey Hadden Leisure Centre in Nottingham for fight night. Jimmy's up against another bad boy Brazilian; Igor Araujo. Igor is a BJJ machine with a stack of submission victories on the European circuit. The place is a hive of activity. Loads of men in black fiddling with the mess of cables and high end TV cameras. Ringside, there are a lot of heavy duty Russians in expensive suits.

This is the first UK show of the self styled 'World Cup of MMA'; The M-1 Challenge. M-1 have brought their product to the East Midlands as a taster to prepare for the launch of an English team next season. The evening drags. The first international challenge sees the Russian Legion team win 4-1 one. Their quartet of victories all come by way of decision as the Russians seem to have forgotten what sport they are taking part in. Round after round of judo scarf holds with no attempt to finish their opponents. Everyone's looking for excitement. Thank god it's Jimmy time.

Igor versus Jimmy is one of three 'superfights' added to the card to pull in the punters. Jimmy gets a rapturous reception. The fans fondly remember his heroic exploits against Nascimento. Jimmy looks in great shape. He's been over in Vegas training at Xtreme Couture. Not cheap, but it's a good investment.

The classic 1970s sitcom Porridge provided one of the most accurate portrayals of the way fight game works. In the episode *The Harder They Fall*, Slade Prison is anticipating the inter wing boxing tournament- with Fletcher's cell mate Lenny Godber the hot favourite. About thirty seconds of the episode features actual fighting, the rest of it is filled with the negotiating and politicking of the money men looking to make a buck. When Fletch is giving Godber his pre-fight rub down, the young Brummie tells him not to worry. The old lag replies: 'It's not the outcome of the fight I'm worried about. It's the outcome of the outcome.' This time, the outcome looks promising for Jimmy. The suits in the room are far bigger players than genial Harry Grout. Guys who can make financial worries go away. There's a wider audience out there too. This kind of exposure can only open doors. One ingredient is vital; 'keep winning'.

Shoot – sprawl – clinch – down - bang – bang – KO. That's the full account of Jimmy's victory over Igor Araujo and, at one minute nineteen seconds, it didn't take much longer than that. Jimmy kept the jiu jitsu black belt out of his comfort zone and took him apart. Wallhead turned to the crowd and shrugged. It was almost like he was apologising for being too good. He clinically executed a game plan in double quick time. Let the good times roll.

The Rough House clan are out in force for Jimmy's next fight, including UFC stars Dan Hardy and Paul Daley and TUF guys Dean Amasinger and Andre Winner. Fighting is the ultimate individual sport but having the backing of a good camp makes a huge difference. We're not in Vegas. We're not in Tokyo. We're in Doncaster. There had been a few more unfortunate outcomes for Jimmy.

The ninth season of The Ultimate Fighter had a twist. The UFC's reality show would pit a team of fighters from the UK against a team from the USA. Try outs were held at Earls Court the month after the Igor fight. A place on TUF was like a golden ticket. Keep your chocolate river; this was a direct route to the bright lights. A six figure contract for the last man standing. The exposure the also rans got guaranteed dough for them in the future. Everyone's a winner.

Jimmy impressed at the auditions. Not surprising, he always did. He was strongly fancied to take the title. 'Keep fighting, keep winning, keep enjoying it.' When the cast was announced- no Jimmy. Rumours abounded. Some said that Jimmy was too quiet and they were looking for someone who would make more entertaining TV. Plenty felt that Jimmy was considered to be too good to be on the show.

Jimmy was immediately installed as clear favourite to take the Welterweight section of the British Fighting Championship; the new project that was going to propel the sport into the mainstream. With the cash prize and the live shows on Bravo, Jimmy was on course to become the most famous MMA fighter in Britain. What could possibly go wrong?

In the first round of the BFC, Jimmy had drawn Fabio Taldo. When the competition went down the toilet, Ultimate Force put the fight on at the Donny Dome. With all the trials and tribulations, Jimmy had been out of the cage for eight months. He needed to fight. 'Keep fighting, keep winning, keep enjoying it.'

Jim comes out looking relaxed as ever. He's got a black stripe dyed into his cropped blonde hair; a last desperate attempt to get noticed perhaps. Fabio Taldo was made for him. I'd seen his last fight. It appeared his game plan had been a piece of paper with heel hook written on it. Styles make fights and Taldo is on a hiding to nothing here. With his textbook sprawl and crisp stand up, Jimmy would have the lad for breakfast.

Fabio starts well. He scores with some sharp leg kicks. It looks like he wants to stand up. His corner seem chilled about the strategy. Another leg kick. Worried glances in the Rough House camp. Jimmy looks out of sorts in there. He attempts to take control and throws a right hand moving forward. Taldo answers with a counter. Jimmy is stopped in his tracks; dazed and unsteady. Ripe for the taking. Jimmy clinches up against the fence, buying time till his senses return. Anxious moments. When your face doesn't fit, 'keep winning' is the only thing that matters. The pair break. Jimmy comes forward. A huge right hook causes Fabio to stumble. He regains his footing only to cop an even bigger one, followed by a third to seal the deal. Fabio crashes face first to the canvas.

Later, Jimmy is all smiles. I ask him if he was worried early on. He laughs it off. Taldo did him a favour. Getting a whack helped to blow away the ring rust. His manager, Ian Dean, is doing the rounds, taking the temperature. Later, he'll head back home and send out the usual emails to the matchmakers of all the major organizations. Details of the picture perfect KO and a clear subtext: How much longer can you ignore this guy? He gets the usual outcome.

Jimmy clocked up another win on Clash of Warriors; partly to keep active and partly to help out a mate. That's the kind of bloke he is. The next test was looming.

KnuckleUp were the latest outfit to crash the UK scene with a plan to take the sport to the next level. They made a grand gesture, booking the luxurious Celtic Manor resort and matching Jimmy against former Cage Rage British Welterweight champion Che Mills. Che is almost a carbon copy of Jimmy; a solid guy with skills who never got the breaks. He'd beaten Marius Zaromskis twice, yet it was the high kicking Lithuanian who got the call to fight in Japan and the States. The gossip was stronger than ever. The winner was going to get a juicy deal with a major promotion. Jimmy and Che, the two nicest guys in the sport. The quiet men who are always overlooked. One of them was going to step up. Jimmy or Che, Che or Jimmy.

BLOODY REVOLUTION

The outcome of the outcome was going to be sweet for one of them. After a gruelling three round war, Jimmy got the nod from the judges.

One month later, on December 21st 2009, it finally happened.

The Bellator press release:

'Adding Jim to our welterweight division is magic for Bellator,' said Bellator founder and CEO Bjorn Rebney. 'As one of Europe's top welterweights, Jim will no doubt use our April tournament on Fox Sports Net to introduce US MMA fans to what European fans already know. Jim is the real deal.'

Signed, sealed and delivered. A spot on the hot, up and coming American promotion. They had a proper TV deal in the States so there would be the chance to attract proper sponsors on top of a healthy purse. Jimmy was going to make his Bellator debut on April 22nd 2010 at the Mohegan Sun Casino in Uncasville, Connecticut against the highly rated Jacob McClintock. What could possibly go wrong?

The keen volcanologists among you will have already guessed the punchline. On Thursday April 15th, British airspace was shut down as a result of an ash cloud emanating from Iceland. The disruption spread across Europe,making transatlantic travel impossible. On Monday April 19th, Bellator announced that Jimmy had been dropped from the Welterweight tournament.

Keep fucking fighting, keep fucking winning, keep fucking enjoying it.

Jimmy was matched up against Mikey Gomez on the Cage Warriors show at the NEC on May 22nd. Gomez was a credible opponent. A win would keep Jimmy in the news. A couple of days before the fight, Gomez pulled out with knee ligament damage. At such short notice, there was only one person to call.

Shaun Lomas enters to the strains of Notorious B.I.G.. 'Juicy' echoes around the empty hall. As usual, he has a huge grin on his face. The king of the journeymen, Lomas fights twice a week most weeks. Muay Thai, kickboxing, unlicensed boxing and now MMA; give him a call and he's there. He's no mug and he can certainly bang, but he's nowhere near Jimmy's class. The fight is second on the bill. Lomas and his kid have come down from Sheffield by rail and they need to get off early to catch their train home.

Jimmy looks like he'd rather be anywhere else. He gets a ripple from the crowd. We'd rather he was somewhere else too. The only atmosphere comes from the small firm of Glaswegians sat behind me, spilling their beer and shouting 'kick his cunt in' every ten seconds. Lomas throws an overhand right and a knee. Jimmy walks through them and takes him down. The contest is effectively over. After dishing out some ground and pound,

BLOODY REVOLUTION

Jimmy takes his back, slaps on the rear naked choke and waits for the inevitable tap. He looks a little embarrassed and can't wait to get out of the cage.

Jimmy heads home. A few days off and it will be back to the grind. Struggling along while he gets while he gets overtaken by fighters who aren't in is league. His time will come. He knows it. He just needs to stick at it.

Keep fighting, keep winning, keep enjoying it.

JAMES

Why do people switch to MMA from other combat sports? Fighters want to test themselves and the cage offers the ultimate challenge for martial artists. Put that cliché to bed and there are more convincing reasons. We live in shallow times. Everybody wants to be famous. Everybody wants to get paid. You see people on telly, you hear rumours about their bank balances and you want in. There's also arrogance. A superiority complex is necessary to succeed as a fighter. You spend your career picking fault in your opponents; working out exactly how you can prove you are better than them. From the first time you walk into a dojo, you are subjected to brainwashing. A man who has dedicated his life to the study of a martial art will repeatedly tell you why his way is better than all the others. Most decisions in the fight game are driven by ego and the love of money.

Muay Thai is the ultimate stand up fighting system. The Science of Eight Limbs was put together by Thais to give them the edge in their battles with Burmese invaders. In these gang rumbles to the death, going to the ground was not an option. Unlike other Eastern martial arts, Thai boxing is bullshit free. The kicks are wonders of physics, pivoting and generating power from the hip to turn the shin into a swinging baseball bat. To supplement what we recognise as conventional punching, elbows are deployed to batter and slice at close range. The cherries on top are the knees; the king of all techniques and surefire rib breakers in the clinch.

One day, someone will write a fascinating book about the history of British Thai boxing. The style arrived in the UK in the 1970s courtesy of a small group of Thai immigrants and a few remarkable British lads who headed in the opposite direction. Remember, this was the pre-internet, pre backpacking, pre working class people ever going anywhere times. A few hardy souls saw pictures in library books and thought: this kung fu is a load of bollocks, I'm going to head off to South East Asia to learn me some real fighting.

From these acorns, a national scene grew. Today, there are Muay Thai gyms across the nation. Participation has boomed in recent years, in no small part due to MMA.

The effectiveness of the techniques has been proven in the cage and lots of kids want in.

The development of professional Thai boxing in the UK has not quite gone to plan. Talk to anyone in the scene and they have the conviction that their sport has not had a fair shake. As they see it, they have put on spectacular fights but do not get any support from TV. They point to the massive success of K-1 kickboxing across Asia and parts of mainland Europe. If Muay Thai got the same push it would soon become a smash hit. The logic is sound, but ignores a number of issues that hold the sport back.

Everything that is right and wrong about the scene was on display on November 26th 2006. Muay Thai Super-fights, live at Wolverhampton Civic Hall. Top of the bill was Peter Crooke in his farewell bout against Sakmong-kol- a legend of the sport. The other featured fights were a roll call of the star names of UK Thai boxing. Men like: Liam Harrison, Andy Thrasher, Christian Di Paolo, Andy Howson and Damien Trainor. Many were title holders, which brings us to problem number one; too many belts. One of the most eagerly awaited contests featured two fighters who both held a version of the Commonwealth title. It was common to see world title fights on UK cards, few of which deserved the name. The various sanctioning bodies played petty political games that rewarded the undeserving and devalued the cheap, gaudy straps bearing their logos.

BLOODY REVOLUTION

One of the things I love about UK Muay Thai community is their steadfast defence of the sport's traditions. Fighters come into the ring wearing ceremonial garlands round their necks and mongkol head bands. Many also wear the impractical kruang ruang armbands around their biceps.

Before the fight, it's time to dance. An individual will have his own version of the ram muay, but most follow the same template. Starting from his own corner, the fighter walks round the ring, dragging a foot across the canvas. This dates back to the olden days. Thais would fight to the death in rings made from dried elephant dung and fighters would check for protruding sharp objects hidden by unscrupulous adversaries. It also has the significance of sealing off the ring to evil spirits. When you reach your opponent's corner, you will always get a big cheer for a theatrical stamp of the foot. The boxer then kneels and performs a quasi religious ritual before standing. This is enough for many, but there is the option to freestyle-usually an exaggerated demonstration of physical prowess like pretending to fire an arrow at your opponent or stealing his treasure chest. I find the whole thing captivating. A fighter's ram muay gives clues to his approach and state of mind. Watching an artist like Richard Cadden dance can be as entertaining as watching him bust heads. You may well think it sounds like a load of pretentious bullshit. If you want to meet like minded people, pop into the packed bar between fights at your local Muay Thai show.

All of the prelims are backed by traditional Thai wood-wind music. When the action starts, a more up tempo tune kicks in. Music while you fight is the norm for anyone with experience of training at a traditional Thai gym. For newcomers, it can be distracting to say the least. The most colourful description of the woodwind band music I have heard is: 'it sounds like gang of stray cats being tied up with rubber bands then raped with a dentist's drill'.

A good crowd turned up at Wolverhampton; around 1,500. The cream of the crop were on show. Skillful, well prepared athletes representing the nation's top camps. The watchword of the Thai boxing brethren is respect. Not respect in its contemporary, twisted, 'I've got a massive car and gun innit' form. Real respect. Fighters go out of their way thank each other for their efforts before and during a fight. A defeated boxer will carry the man who has just kicked the living shit out of him around the ring. Humble is close behind respectful as the greatest compliment you can pay a Thai boxer. The crowd lap it up. The stacked card delivered with all the fights living up to expectations.

James McSweeney entered the hall. The mood changed instantly. Announced as James 'Machine' McSweeney, he milked his entrance to the max. On the stage, he stood in a long black dressing gown, snarling and banging his gloves together. All around the auditorium, people turned to their neighbours and muttered variations on the phrase 'what a prick'. Most of the crowd didn't have a clue who he was. James had not been mentioned in the publicity for the evening and he wasn't featured on the poster. This was dislike at first sight. James did not perform a ram muay, preferring to continue with his looking mean activities instead. Across the ring, his Eastern European opponent looked nervous.

Within ten seconds of the opening bell, the fight was over. Minimal feeling out then WHACK. McSweeney's shinbone connects to the skull and the other guy drops like he's been shot. There's nothing in the wide world of sports like a head kick KO. The crowd explode with the sheer visceral power of the experience.

In a split second, they see that the lad is not moving. The medics dash in. A concerned hush falls over the hall. Everyone is concerned. Everyone except James. High on power, he celebrates. With the adrenaline still pumping, he lets it all hang out. As an MMA fan, I recognize what happened next as a homage to the former UFC 205 lb champion Tito 'The Huntington Beach Bad Boy' Ortiz. To the Muay Thai purists, it was sacrilegious. McSweeney ostentatiously mimes the marking out and digging of a grave.

After the stunned silence, outrage erupts. Abuse and booing. This is unheard of at a Thai show. When the KO victim is helped to his feet, he is cheered to the rafters.

There is no let up in the James baiting. A group of his supporters at ringside give some back. The lay out of the Civic means that the majority of the crowd are upstairs in the balcony seats. From the back a chant starts. In an instant, the whole room joins in.

- YOU FAT BASTARD, YOU FAT BASTARD.

A couple of plastic pint pots fly over the balcony towards the ring. The chant gets louder. This is unprecedented. It's like the Wimbledon Centre Court singing 'You're gonna get your fucking heads kicked in'. James has no future in UK Muay Thai.

The switch to MMA was a no brainer. There were plenty of others who had gone before. Alistair Overeem and Cro-Cop were big in Japan. In the UFC, Cheick Kongo and Antoni Hardonk were making a decent living. European kickboxers could hang with the best of them in the cage. Was James up to that standard? Who knows?

When it comes to empire building, misinformation and pure bullshit for profit, kickboxing and MMA are blood brothers. James claims to have well over 100 wins and string of championship belts; certainly believable in the crazy world of kickboxing. McSweeney had trained at the toughest gyms in Holland so he had seen the other converts first hand.

In the Netherlands, the public have embraced the K-1 style- selling out the Amsterdam Arena on a regular basis. Classicists scoff at the absence of elbow strikes, minimal clinchwork and lack of screeching music, labelling it Muay Thai lite, but it had been hugely successful. After seeing the best in the flesh, James was convinced he could match them.

The crossover stars had something else in common with James. Overeem, Cro-Cop, Kongo, Hardonk: all Heavyweights. In every combat sport, the Heavyweights are the worst of the bunch in terms of entertainment. Slow and heavy footed, they look like featherweights fighting underwater, but they have a couple of strong selling points.

In boxing, the Heavyweight division has its own mythology, with the world champ having the unofficial title of baddest man on the planet (in the dim, distant days when there was only one world champ). They also hit the hardest. The sight of a normal size man getting robbed of his senses is spectacular. Seeing an 18 stone guy getting toppled by a concussive KO is off the charts.

In MMA, Heavyweight has never been the marquee division. The initial UFC was open weight and proved that a smaller man with superior skills could beat a big man. When the sport was courting respectable opinion in order to gain acceptance, weight classes were introduced.

As MMA developed, a new generation of strikers proved that they could confound the wrestlers and grapplers. Sprawl and brawl was born. Power hitters like Chuck Liddell and Wanderlei Silva perfected the sprawl to stuff takedowns then dished out the punishment on the feet. As this pair electrified the fans, the Heavyweight division was a charismatic slugger free zone. The qualifications for getting a UFC contract appeared to consist of weighing over 205 lbs and having a pulse. The stand up was plodding, the grappling sloppy.

James must have seen an open goal. MMA was the world's fastest growing sport and his weight class was weak and crying out for new blood. Like I said, the switch was a no brainer.

Cage Rage snapped James up. He was introduced to the Wembley masses in a three round kickboxing match against an over the hill Michael McDonald. McSweeney showed some nice touches on his way to the decision win. In his first London MMA fight, there were flashes of a ground game as James overcame Mark 'The Cannon' Buchanan in 90 seconds.

Although they were Cockney to the core, Cage Rage often looked East for inspiration. As well as welcoming a number of refugees from Pride, they shared that promotion's love of a freak show- a contest that featured unusual human specimens. The bigger, the better. For his third fight, Cage Rage had matched James with Robert Paczkow. The pre-publicity described Paczkow as a leading Polish Sumo wrestler. Every preview of the event poked fun at his credentials. Surely becoming a leading Polish Sumo is not a hard task. Robert was a big fish in a small pond. A huge, flabby, hairy backed one; he showed every ounce of the 330 lbs he'd weighed in at.

The fat bloke sat next to me was delighted to have found one of the few people in the world he could look down on. He yelled:

-You fat smelly cunt.

Harsh, but it passed on the grounds of fair comment. Paczkow's belly hung over the waistband of a pair of boxing shorts that had seen better days. Fatso and his mates went wild for McSweeney, who was now trading as 'The Hammer'. He was led in by a rapper called Shizzio- a man blessed with a name that is almost an accurate review. Shiz spat out lyrics that testified to the meanness and potency of McSweeney. The man himself followed with a scowl. Fatso and his gang were well into it- shouting the vilest encouragement possible to their home- boy. They were looking forward to the kickboxing Brit standing off the sluggish Eastern European and tearing him a new arsehole. Pick the fat bastard off with single shots for a while then move in and finish him. Sort of bullfighting featuring a morbidly obese bull with a budget haircut.

This was the perfect fight for James. The nationalistic slant meant the whole crowd was on his side. He would surely have the speed and footwork to evade the Pole's clutches. Cane the fat bloke and move on up.

About ten seconds in, it all went pear shaped. James threw a Superman punch. Robert pushed him as his feet were off the canvas and it was all over. Well not literally, but as good as. There is little you can do if a 23 stone bloke with some grappling smarts decides to lay on you. James struggled manfully to no avail. After two minutes, he tapped to a bit of choke and a lot of smother.

Fatso next to me let rip.

- You facking cant. You useless facking cant.

I couldn't tell if he was shouting at James or the winner. The fight had genuinely upset him and his mates. The bull winning is not in the script. Their level of insecurity was so high they were after blood. Being first scapegoat in line, I made a tactical withdrawal to the bar. James and I had learnt a lesson: Never underestimate the power of Polish Sumo.

How was he punished for this slip up? With a title shot of course. Mustapha al Turk was a league above a novice like James. Mus took him down and had his way with him on the deck till the ref stepped in. James went off and picked up a win at FX3 in Reading. He had given himself half a chance of another run with Cage Rage- but Cage Rage was done. The UK's most over the top promotion disappeared. Hooking up with the American money of ProElite was supposed to take Cage Rage up a level. Instead, it dragged it down the toilet. ProElite went tits up and Cage Rage was no more. The final show under that banner was Cage Rage 28- V.I.P.. James knocked out an out of shape Roman Webber within ten seconds of the opening bell.

The evening was billed as an exclusive, high class affair- but most people sussed that it was a preamble to Cage Rage R.I.P.. Wembley had been swapped for the Troxy in Limehouse. Even without the interference of the bungling Yanks, this move may have been inevitable. There were often wide open spaces in the stands at the Arena and many of the bums on seats were there courtesy of freebies. The writing was on the wall.

December 6th, 2008. Less than three months after the V.I.P. show, the go go girls are grinding their spandex booties all around the Troxy. Every spare art deco fitting has a scantily clad lass hanging from it. Cage Rage is dead, long live Ultimate Challenge. Dave O'Donnell had weathered the shit storm and kept MMA alive in the capital. Live for the punters and live nationwide thanks to a TV deal. OK, it was only Nuts TV, but it was the kind of exposure all his rivals would sell their grannies for.

Top of the bill was a match for the Ultimate Challenge Heavyweight title: James McSweeney v Neil 'The Goliath' Grove. Grove had burst onto the Cage Rage scene with a couple of lightning fast demolition jobs. In his subsequent fights, his limitations had been exposed and the hype around him was dying down. Grove was a name, but James had to fancy the job. If he could stay away from the big punches for a while and wear out the big South

African, surely he would be able to take advantage later on.

The main event approached. I was high and intoxicated. Literally high up, standing behind the back row of the Troxy's steeply tiered circle seats. A perfect view- those 1930s bods knew a thing or two about building a theatre. Literally intoxicated. Dave had a reputation as a good matchmaker, but pull outs had interfered with his balancing act. Of the other ten bouts on the cobbled together card, eight finished in the first. When live TV is a factor, the needs of the punters in the house are rated way below the needs of the punters on the settee. Long gaps appeared in the schedule. I plugged them with plastic bottles of Stella and went with the flow. No way was James versus Grove worthy of any kind of title, but it should produce some fireworks. Up in the cheap seats, Grove had a sizeable following- a quaint mob decked out in matching club T-shirts. They started to get vocal and ramped up the atmosphere.

From the speakers; the sounds of growling dogs. The track kicks in. It's DMX, the patron saint of ill judged ring walks. James enters the fray wearing a mask. Heads shake from pity. Once again, James is losing friends and alienating people with his Buford the Bully shenanigans. In contrast, Grove enters smiling and respectfully folds his black belt and gi jacket before entering the cage.

The action commences and the crowd is raising the roof. I'm starting to believe. Showing he's not learnt his lesson, James opens with a Superman punch. This time he gets away with it. James looks sharp. Grove gets the message, grabs hold of his man and dumps him to the canvas with the ferocity of a Jamaican domino player. From his back, James works himself into some nice positions but hasn't got the nous to find a finish. Neil sits in his guard. James edges his heels up the South African's back. When Grove lets a punch go, he leans forward and leaves himself vulnerable. James slips his calf round the back of the exposed neck. The other leg is in position. A triangle choke is there for the taking. In a split second, the snare will tighten and the game will be up. The lads in matching T-shirts can't look. Their boy is toast.

Time stands still in the cage. James doesn't apply the coup de grace. Grove appears unaware of his imminent demise and makes no attempt to escape. His fans scream: 'triangle, triangle'; a word that really doesn't lend itself to yelling. With a head full of Belgian lager, the effect is bordering on surreal. One of the T-shirt crew turns to his brothers.

- Shut up or McSweeney will hear you.

No need to worry mate. From the back row of the Troxy, no one can hear you scream. The moment drags on and on. It is obvious that the two title contenders have no idea what a crucial point the fight has reached. Meanwhile, the lads in the cheap seats are acutely aware and going ballistic.

- Triangle, facking triangle.

Next to the bar, a couple of pissheads have been abandoned by whoever dragged them along against their will. They are bemused by scene and embark on some cutting edge satire.

- Square, rectangle, facking rhombus.

Delighted with themselves, the pair turn their backs on the madness to order another Stella. Still no decisive move. Everyone is looking next them, making sure they're not imagining it. All get the same disbelieving shrug of the shoulders. Excitement has become bafflement. On and on and on. There is going to be a second round.

In the break, a guy I've never set eyes on before yells in my face.

- What the fuck is wrong with them? It was there. The triangle.

He looks desperate. He needs reassurance. All I can give him is a nod and a weak smile.

James staggers out for the second. The gas arrow is close to zero. 'The Goliath' pushes him over. No finesse, no skill, just another great big feller picking on James. Grove lets him have it. James has no answer to the ground and pound. The ref waves it off. The joint erupts in praise of the victor. James takes it all in good spirit, but he must realize the game is up.

I slip out into the cold East London night before the belt is awarded. I've got a train to catch and I don't really want to be part of the charade. Don't get me wrong; I'd enjoyed the fight. The atmosphere had been ace but, no matter how drunk I am, I won't kid myself that I'd seen a contest worthy of being called a championship fight. This has to be the high watermark for both the winner and James. On that evidence, neither is ever going to progress further in the sport. The Troxy is the end of the line.

Ten days after the fight, Fighters Only broke the news that Neil Grove had signed a contract with the UFC. A few months later, James McSweeney was announced as a cast member on the tenth season of the UFC's reality TV show The Ultimate Fighter.

Some guys have all the luck

TELLY

-Rag it, fucking rag it.

Despite the boisterous encouragement coming from the English camp, Sergey Kornev chose not to break the arm of his opponent. The Russian was playing with him, building up to a brutal neck crank. To a man, the English contingent screwed up their faces in sympathy. As fighters, they knew exactly how that felt. That's why they had the licence to speak freely. Every sub attempt drew a shout of 'rag it' or 'rip the fucker off'. Some of the foreigners' records were ridiculed:

- If he's got 15 wins, he must be counting fights with his little cousin in the garage.

Any suspiciously developed body prompted a discussion of what cocktail of steroids its owner favoured. In turn, each would then tell a horror story about juicers they had come across in their careers, ranging from the usual nightmare roid tales to even more nightmarish yarns about guys so full of painkillers they would not tap; even when their foot had almost been ripped from their leg. Of course, this was all strictly off the record. Team England were demob happy and having a laugh.

The heckling seemed out of place in the sedate surroundings. We were in Studio 22 at the Hilversum Media Park. There were about another 100 people scattered across the seats and the atmosphere was flat.

M-1 Global had run into some scheduling problems and had taken decisive action. The six remaining team matches (a total of 30 individual bouts) of the 2009 M-1 Challenge were to take place over two evenings in a Dutch TV studio. Team England had done their job on the Saturday. They arrived knowing they had to beat Team Spain 5-0 to stand a chance of progressing to the semi finals in Rostov-on-Don, Russia. Even though they had two inexperienced lads filling gaps in the ranks, they had completed the whitewash. In the next match, France had lost 3-2 against Japan which meant that England had topped their group.

After a moderate (by Amsterdam standards) night out, the lads were back. In theory, they were running the rule over their semi final opponents, The Russian Legion, but the vibe was more school trip than scouting mission.

Before the Legion's clash with Team Turkey, there was a meaningless match between Japan and Spain. The Spanish team were on the end of some piss taking due to their perceived arrogance. They had turned up to the weigh in with nine guys. When challenged, the Spanish Light heavyweight explained that he was going to fight on both nights. When England's Tom Blackledge head kicked the man in question out cold in nine seconds, he required medical attention and the Sunday night line up was re-jigged.

Team Spain were a soft target. The Russians were not. Their Lightweight came out, picked up his Turkish opposite number and slammed him head first onto the ground, knocking him spark out. The state of the art big screen slow motion made it worse every time. The vertebrae in the neck looked set to pop out of his skin on impact and he had the vacant eyes of a traffic warden when he came to rest on the canvas. I was looking around for authentic reaction but was met by brave faces. However hard everyone was trying to look, you could feel the relief when he finally stood up.

One after another, the Russians came out and each rag dolled a Turk into submission. There were holes though. Their stand up was pedestrian and there was no way they could mug off the English by throwing overhand rights that turned into single leg shots. This was 2009, not 1993. The consensus view: good but beatable. Basically, the standard fighter response to anybody.

BLOODY REVOLUTION

The crowd started to swell as some locals turned up for the Benelux v USA East fights. It was the first time all weekend that the small hall was even half full.

I'd had hopes that a decent number of UK fans would take advantage of the budget airlines and get behind the team but it never happened. I was the only British writer covering the event and the only recognisable Team England fan the night before had been Paul Kelly. Unfortunately, he'd got the times mixed up and arrived when the England match was over, but it's the thought that counts.

M-1 have cottoned onto an underlying truth about MMA fans; they are the ultimate armchair supporters. Most have never actually seen the sport in the flesh and are content with second hand screen violence.

The M-1 mega taping made sense. Even if they sold out a decent sized hall, M-1 would only be making a few grand on the gate. Their real target audience are those who watch the M-1 Challenge in the 80 countries around the world in which it is televised. Handy, bitesized chunks of cage fighting with flags and stuff for those too dim to choose who to root for without a hint. If you film your fights in a TV studio, you can guarantee premium quality for your real consumers. The live crowd are merely there as background artistes to add some colour. You could argue this was true of any modern sport, but MMA's relationship with TV runs particularly deep.

The UFC started out as a TV special that spawned a series of sequels and eventually morphed into a sport. The promotion staged its events in halls out of the reach of regulators and put them out on pay per view. No holds barred fighting was an outlaw activity that most considered a sordid spectacle rather than a bona fide sport.

In 2000, New Jersey became the first state athletic commission to regulate MMA. Other states followed their lead, but the wilderness years had left the UFC finances in a sorry state.

The following year, the promotion was bought by Frank and Lorenzo Fertitta of Station Casinos. The brothers, along with a mate called Dana White, set up Zuffa LLC as a parent company to control their MMA interests. Under new ownership, the UFC began to look more respectable, but it was still far from profitable. $34 million is the number usually bandied about as what it cost Zuffa to keep the UFC afloat. They were in a hole. And then TV saved them.

As a final throw of the dice, the Zuffa decided to jump on the reality television bandwagon. In 'The Ultimate Fighter' a group of fighters would be locked away in a house; only let out to train and to fight in a knockout tournament. The winner would be rewarded with a six figure contract to fight in the UFC. After unsuccessfully shopping the idea round the networks, Zuffa did a deal with cable channel Spike TV- a men and motors type of outfit. The catch- the Fertittas had to throw another $10 million into the money pit to cover production costs.

The Ultimate Fighter debuted in 2005 and caught on fast. It had a great cast, including: Diego Sanchez (Mr Intensity), Chris Leben (lovable rogue with a hair trigger) and Josh Koscheck (arrogant arsehole). Another star in the making was the Lex Luther-esque Dana White, whose 'Do you wanna be a fucking fighter?' speech became an instant classic.

Ratings were good. The live finale was exceptional. Forrest Griffin and Stephan Bonnar produced one of the all time great slug fests. Folk history has it that phones and computers buzzed as people urged their friends to switch on Spike as the battle raged. By the end of the fight, the UFC had conquered North America. Business boomed, Zuffa blossomed into a billion dollar concern and MMA meant something to the man on the street. To get the crowd going at UFC events, they show a lengthy highlight video immediately before the main card goes live. It concludes with Griffin v Bonnar whacking the hell out of each other to Baba O'Reilly by The Who. Griffin v Bonnar was the game changer. For MMA, it was Elvis on the Ed Sullivan Show and the Sex Pistols abusing Bill Grundy rolled into one.

The Ultimate Fighter has boosted the popularity of MMA in the UK too. Most of the new wave of fans cottoned onto the sport because of the seemingly constant reruns of UFC highlights on Bravo. The channel picked up The Ultimate Fighter and struck gold when Michael Bisping and Ross Pointon were selected for the third season. Stoke native Pointon was a TV natural, handling intense situations with a laid back attitude and a winning smile. Bisping matched Pointon for wise cracks and beat all his opponents in the cage to win a UFC deal.

Bisping returned as a coach for season nine when the format was shaken up to make it a contest between teams from the UK and the USA. By this time, there was an anti-Brit and anti-Bisping backlash from a sizeable number of American fans. The internet forum dwellers had decided that Bisping had been matched easy and had benefited from soft judging in his UFC career. Other UK fighters were guilty by association and cynics claimed that a deliberately weak US team had been selected to make the Brits look good.

The UFC had earmarked Britain as the ideal base for its invasion of Europe and needed new local heroes to put on their cards. TUF 9 Lightweight finalists Ross Pearson and Andre Winner had been identified as hot prospects by UK scene watchers and the series gave them a helping hand to the big time.

The following season also had British interest. James McSweeney got a spot and was picked first by his coach and close friend Rashad Evans. The coach of the other team, Evans' arch enemy Rampage Jackson, called up his Wolfslair team mate Tom Blackledge to help lick his lads into fighting shape. It had not aired yet when we were in

BLOODY REVOLUTION

Hilversum and Tom was sworn to secrecy about the outcome. In this internet age, it's easy enough to find out what's happened if you want, but no-one's that bothered. Tom wasn't the only media darling associated with the England team. The recently retired Ian Butlin was along to assist with coaching duties. He impressed the M-1 bosses and would go on to become the promotion's TV commentator.

The neatly top and tailed M-1 TV show was first shown on Bravo in the UK before moving to the Extreme Sports channel. About time I'd say. Most 'extreme sports' are fundamentally about posh knobheads dressing in bright clothing, jumping off something and shouting 'Weeeeeee-Look at me'. MMA is a truly extreme sport where you put it all on the line- but you do it in a backstreet sweatshop and don't get to pose about in front of lasses called Tamara.

The M-1 Challenge is a polished product, but it is little more than a space-filler in the TV schedules. This is the fate of most excursions into television by shows featuring UK talent. The exception was Cage Rage. Those guys had it all: shows broadcast live in a prime Saturday night slot on Sky Sports. At last, the British public would get to see domestic MMA. The boom was coming, the prophecy was true.

Cage Rage on Sky didn't work out. Fans of the product will tell you that Sky didn't get behind it and were under pressure from boxing interests to drop it. The other side of the story is that tacky production values and too much

Cockney gurning made the show an embarrassment. Whatever the reason, Cage Rage did not catch on with the viewers and it was unceremoniously dumped. The show ended up on Nuts TV, as did its later incarnation Ultimate Challenge. When that channel bit the dust, it took live UK MMA with it.

Ultimate Challenge made it back to Sky, but only as an edited highlights package on Wednesday nights after the event. Other UK shows have fared little better. Cage Gladiators had a deal with ITV4 that showcased the best of the action from their Olympia shows. The restrained presentation got a thumbs up from fans but the show was stuck in a graveyard slot then killed off because of the cutbacks at ITV. KnuckleUp also sneaked on to Sky, but did not really make a ripple.

If you can be bothered, you can usually find some cage fighting somewhere in the listings. Tucked away in the nether regions of the TV planner are seemingly random chunks of MMA. At any given time on any given day, you can be sure that the outdoor King of the Cage where it pisses it down is playing somewhere on a UK TV channel.

For a while, TWC (The Wrestling Channel later The Fight Network UK) was the place to see UK MMA. All the top shows would be featured in a regular UK MMA hour. The channel went off air late in 2008. The shows on TWC were shown without introduction and totally out of context. All the footage was courtesy of the promoters themselves. From the start, shows had been filmed for production of DVDs. Often with rock bottom production values, they were of little interest to anyone except people who had fought on the show. The short sighted desire to protect DVD sales has meant that UK promoters have been slow to embrace the internet. Obviously, the fans have not, so you get the bizarre situation where shows hoard their film in the vain hope of flogging it for £20 a pop while YouTube is full of grainy phone footage. Nobody is making proper money and the shows come over as cheap and grubby. But it's the way it's always been so that's how it must stay.

The 600 lb gorilla in the corner is the UFC. All of their shows are available live on subscription sports channels. First on Setanta, then ESPN and there's a strong suspicion Sky Sports will snap it up eventually (they are the current home of The Ultimate Fighter). Few doubt that the long game is a switch to the pay per view model they operate in America. I can't see that ever working satisfactorily over here, but I've never built a billion dollar business.

A new approach came with the launch of BAMMA (British Association of Mixed Martial Arts). The promotion's backers were Giant Film & TV. Giant dipped their toe into the MMA pool when they collaborated with Cage Rage on Fighting Hurts, an achingly low budget Ultimate Fighter type series on Nuts TV. Like everyone else in the game, they saw the potential and threw in their lot with Dave

O'Donnell. From day one, BAMMA were aiming to put together a show for fans nationwide rather than building from a regional base. They were TV people looking to produce a TV friendly show. They even brought in proper celeb Christian O'Connell for interview duty.

Amid the traditional unsubstantiated rumours of skull-duggery, the first BAMMA show was announced in June 2009, shortly after the collapse of the proposed British Fighting Championships. Like the BFC, BAMMA proposed a knockout tournament to determine the best fighter in each weight class. The first instalment of BAMMA 'The Fighting Premiership' took place on Saturday June 27th at the tiny Room by the River in London. The show featured the semi finals of the Light-weight, Welterweight and Middleweight divisions. There was a little bitching about the event, but there could be no doubt about the calibre of talent on show- the likes of Che Mills, Denniston Sutherland, John Phillips, Tim Radcliffe, Eugene Fadiora and Abdul Mohamed were a match for anyone domestically. Highlights of the card made jolly Sunday night viewing for the Bravo audience and everything looked set for them to kick on.

The other semis were scheduled for August 15th with the finals a month later. At the end of July, Dave O'Donnell ended his relationship with BAMMA and publicly voiced his displeasure about the way they did business. A deafening silence came from the BAMMA camp, but the word that their second show was off leaked out from various interested sources. UK MMA promotion overstretches and bites the dust is not a new headline and everyone assumed that was the end of that. How wrong we were.

Whispers about a BAMMA 2 started doing the rounds in late 2009 and the show was officially announced for February 13th 2010. The Fighting Premiership idea was dead and the new show included two fights for the vacant Featherweight and Lightweight titles.

BAMMA 2 was held at the legendary Roundhouse in Chalk Farm, NW1. Rob Sinclair and German prodigy Alan Omer took the belts and Icelandic grappling star Gunnar Nelson put in a shift that suggested his billing as the second coming of Jesus Christ was justified. The TV package was more polished than the first effort. Had we finally got a promotion capable of taking UK MMA to the mainstream?

To be continued....

CAREER OPPORTUNITIES

UFC 89
National Indoor Arena, Birmingham
18th October 2008

It was beautiful autumn evening in Birmingham. Outside the National Indoor Arena, Neil Wain's supporters were bullish ahead of UFC 89. Most of them had a decent bet on. As they held a minority view, they had enjoyed some fancy odds. Against my better judgement, I'd joined them. The 11/2 I'd got on Betfair seemed about right.

I'd had the Sherdog roundtable on the iPod on the trip down and heard unanimous agreement that Shane Carwin was a monster; one of the new breed of superhulk wrestlers who were going to own the UFC Heavyweight division for the foreseeable future. Neil was a stepping stone on the road to better things. I got all that... but Wainy's people had a belief. It was infectious.

BLOODY REVOLUTION

Inside the arena, I got held up by a masked man. Dan 'The Outlaw' Hardy's gimmick was a Wild West baddie neckerchief across the face. Ian Dean from his management team modelled a sponsored replica and was dishing spares out to the fans. We had a quick chat on gambling matters. I'd piled on Hardy at 7/4. Unbelievable value. All the American experts had picked Gono- singing the same old song about Brit's being overrated. Hopefully, we'd be able to cash in on their ignorance.

Neil Wain and Dan Hardy were both making their UFC debuts. This was the promised land for every pro- a spot on the big show with the big crowds and the chance of big money down the line.

Nine months earlier, I'd seen Neil Wain from a distance at UFC 80 in Newcastle. He was up in the stands, sat next to Dave Mangham from Ultimate Force, and I was down in the floor seats. Neil had just signed his contract then. Nobody took any notice of him. He was surrounded by armchair UFC fans who wouldn't know a small hall fighter from Adam. I remember thinking- this will be his last time coming to a gig like this without getting mobbed by spotty herberts in T-shirts splattered with skulls and chains.

Another homegrown Heavyweight was on the card that night. Colin Robinson got chopped down by the Dutch kickboxer Antoni Hardonk in just 17 seconds of the opening round; making his UFC record 0-2. After the caning, his eyes had a haunted look blown up on the big screen. Some of Big C's best recent performances had been in the North East, on Total Combat and Strike 'n' Submit, but that meant nothing to the Metro Arena day trippers who heckled his post fight interview. He was on his way back down to the minors and everyone knew it.

In initial talks, a young lad called Cain Velasquez was mooted as a suitable match for Neil Wain, but the Yorkshireman was eventually confirmed as Hardonk's next opponent in June at UFC 85 at the O2 in London.

The confidence from his camp was overwhelming. I went over to Germany to see some of the other Doncaster lads fight and they were all counting the days to Wainy's explosion onto the world scene. He was a natural. He hit harder than anyone else. He was going to stuff the critics' words down their throats. And there were plenty of critics-shouting how he was undeserving compared to.... (insert name of their fighter). I interviewed Neil in the run up to the fight. He was almost apologetic about his meteoric rise.

Neil Wain's MMA career began when he made a passing comment to his girlfriend about boxing when he was a kid. She said she'd have liked to seen him fight and he sorted out a bout on his mate Dave Mangham's show. Neil did little training, a couple of weeks in the gym to get his hands going, and wore a black rash guard for fights to cover up his less than buff upper body. Five fights and five first round demolitions won him a golden ticket.

BLOODY REVOLUTION

Everything I knew about the sport told me that Neil wasn't ready, but the conviction of his team was impossible to resist. His nickname was Old Skool and it perfectly summed up his no frills style.

Everyone wanted Wainy to do well. He was the archetypal working class hero; eager to talk about his family and totally not arsed about the prospect of stardom. Wainy has a strange charisma that makes everyone who meets him a believer. The heavies stink. Maybe he can go in there and make some hay. Standing a mere 5 ft 10 " and tipping the scales at over 17 stone, Neil made an unlikely elite sportsman, but that only added to his appeal. He was the everyman: the bloke in the pub, the feller at the match.

Whispers from the gym added to the legend. His short limbs made him impossible to submit. His power was so profound, nobody could trade with him and live to tell the tale. Hardonk wouldn't know what had hit him.

Hardonk got lucky. Neil suffered a broken nose in training and had to pull out. The next time I saw his team was at Cage Warriors in Nottingham. They told me that Neil was going to fight at UFC 89 against Shane Carwin. I tried to stop an involuntary grimace spreading across my face. Carwin had never been beyond the first round and was being touted as the future of the Heavyweights by sections of the American press. The Doncaster contingent were unconcerned. If you're from the North of England, you're used to being talked down to by people who don't have a clue. Wainy was going to get the job done. No bother.

Dan Hardy had taken a totally different route to the Octagon. One day someone, probably Dan himself, will write a great book about his rise up the ranks.

Dan Hardy- Life as an Outlaw will tell of how he started out in the trad arts; taking up TKD as an ankle biter and even having a spell at the Shaolin temple. When he decided to test himself in full contact competition, Dan became a key member of Team Rough House in his native Nottingham. Dan was never a huge ticket seller, but he had potential and ambition. He juggled training with a job at a leisure centre. His wages and leave days were saved up to fund trips to America where he would hone his skills in the best gyms. The savvy Cage Warriors matchmaker picked fights that would move him along at the right pace.

In 2007, he upped his profile with a couple of wins in Japan. Dan was rated as the top Welterweight in the nation by many. His only serious challengers to that title were his team mates Paul Daley and Jimmy Wallhead.

It wasn't only about results. Dan was a complete package: the dyed hair and co-ordinated shorts, the flashy Muay Thai, the confidence verging on arrogance. He was a face in Japan and the UFC were shopping for UK talent. One way or another- Dan was going global.

The announcement came at the Doncaster Dome- the scene of Wainy's greatest hits. Dan overcame the German submission specialist Daniel Weichel. After the fight, his management entered the cage and let the crowd in on the secret. Dan been snapped up by the UFC. There was applause. The general feeling was: about time too. His first opponent was to be the Pride veteran Akihiro Gono. Dan headed to Xtreme Couture in Vegas to tune up. He appeared on the right podcasts and gave cheeky interviews to the right blogs. In the weeks leading up to show time, everything seemed on track.

Neil Wain is in the cage and ready to rumble. As he shakes out, he still cuts an anonymous figure. His entrance was literally unheralded. The first four bouts of the evening all went into the third round so Wain and Carwin had their ring walks cut to stop the undercard from running over into the time allotted for the featured, televised bouts. Neil looked different. He'd cropped his hair to the bone and, for the first time in his pro career, he was fighting without his shirt on.

Wainy comes out shooting. Carwin has his hands down. Wainy clips him. The pair trade heavy shots. This is it baby. This is Wainy's kind of fight. Carwin has lost his mind. He's believed his own hype and underestimated the Yorkshire lad. Carwin comes to his senses and takes Neil down. The fight is over. When a muscular 19 stone man with a lifetime of wrestling behind him has you on your back, you are at his mercy. Carwin lands punches to Neil's head till the ref has had enough. He waves it off. 91 seconds into his UFC debut, Neil Wain has tasted defeat for the first time.

England Belongs to Me by the cult Oi! band Cock Sparrer blares out. The quick end to the Carwin/Wain fight means that Dan Hardy gets his ring walk. The Outlaw's Mohawk is a proud bright red and his eyes burn over the top of his mask. His three man corner team includes team mate Jim Wallhead- always the bridesmaid.

Akihiro Gono raises the stakes. He enters in a figure hugging Lycra suit, shades and an exaggerated cartoon quiff wig. Two identically dressed Japanese men follow him. Halfway through the hall, the trio halt then break into a dance routine in time to a cheesy Jap pop accompaniment. The crowd laugh as one. No matter how much you yearn for the sport to be taken seriously, you've got to love the Japanese showmanship.

The fight goes as expected. Hardy uses his reach and picks Gono off at range. Gono threatens a little on the deck and catches Dan late on, but it's too little too late. The Hardy connections are sitting down the row from me. I give them a little nod. Dan's first UFC win is in the bag. When Buffer calls the decision, I'm momentarily all at sea. Split decision. For me it was a clear win for Hardy. The panic is only temporary. One rogue makes it 29-28 Gono, the other two judges have actually watched the fight and go 29-28 the other way. I over celebrate the result due to the windfall it will net me from the bookies. The thousands in the NIA give him a nearly as warm reception.

Dan did enough to get on the featured section of the card for his next outing at UFC 95. He repaid the faith of the UFC by delivering a concussive first round KO of Rory Markham. He had the look and the mouth- now he shown the TV fans he had the skills to back it up. Dan had arrived.

In this internet age, you win a lot of instant love if you have a cool haircut and pop sensibilities. It was essential to build upon the adulation. In combat sports, image and the ability to play politics are important tools in a fighter's arsenal. If the many fighters who tell interviewers 'I don't care who I fight next, I'll fight anyone' are telling the truth- they are 24 carat fuckwits.

The Hardy camp had to pick a beatable opponent, secure the fight, sell it and, only then, concentrate on winning it. They selected Marcus Davis, a decent gate-keeper to the upper echelons of the Welterweight division who went by the handle 'The Irish Hand Grenade'. Hardy called him out in public, signed the deal then went to town.

Dan found a photograph of Davis in a borderline camp pose. He posted the snap on the cagewarriors.com internet forum with the prompt: 'Photoshop anyone?' Predictably, the vast majority of the offering depicted Davis as a raving homosexual or a deviant leprechaun.

Davis went off the deep end, giving crazed interviews where he declared his hatred for Hardy.

I caught up with Dan in Doncaster. He was up supporting Jimmy Wallhead at Ultimate Force. The fight was a month away, at UFC 99 in Cologne, and his training camp had moved home for its final stages. Based in LA, he had been training at some of the most famous fight gyms out there. He was a regular on the mat at weed smoking, rock'n'roll guru Eddie Bravo's 10th Planet Jiu Jitsu.

Dan was living the life by now, but he was totally unaffected. He had a kid's enthusiasm when he talked about a spell he'd had brushing up his boxing at the Wild Card gym in Hollywood. How privileged he'd felt to get the chance to do bits of work with Freddie Roach and his awe at the skills and dedication of Manny Pacquiao. When I asked him about the photoshop campaign, he shrugged with a smile. It was part of the game. A bit of a laugh. The fact that Davis had let it get to him was even better.

The photoshop furore brought more attention to the fight. Dan's management even ran a coach to Germany. It went as well as any activity with the instructions 'meet at 4am in King's Cross' can. Dan won on points and moved into the title picture.

His next fight was an eliminator against Mike Swick at UFC 105. Dan had made it to co-main event status. He overcame Swick and earned a title shot against Georges

BLOODY REVOLUTION

St. Pierre, most people's idea of the best pound for pound fighter in the world. Knowing that Dan could sell a fight, the UFC put together three Primetime preview shows that followed the fighters in the run up to the contest.

The fight itself was one sided. The British wrestling deficit exposed by the best exponent of wrestling in MMA. GSP won every round convincingly to retain his title, but that doesn't take away from Hardy's achievement. He was the first Brit to challenge for a title and had established himself as a genuine star. With time on his side and a reputation for hyping a fight- he can come again. He's living the life and loving the life.

I was up till 5am watching Dan's frustration. The next evening, I was in Leeds for Fightstars; the touring show for up and comers run by Chris Zorba. I nipped into Subway for a pre-show feed and bumped into the lads from Manvers Fight Factory. Over footlongs and Sprite, we discussed the early morning action from New Jersey.

Apart from Dan v GSP, the most significant fight at UFC 111 had been Shane Carwin's first round demolition of Frank Mir to take the UFC Interim Heavyweight title. Playing the part of the shrewd fight writer, I began holding court on the tactical naivety of Mir. I switched to explaining in detail the phenomenal punching power of Carwin. How you just can't imagine what it's like to take a shot off someone that size. I tailed off and returned to my sandwich. I realised that one of my audience members knew exactly what it was like to take Shane Carwin's hardest punches.

Neil Wain's UFC career was one and out. His minute and a half of fame made it onto the live broadcast as filler and that was that. Wainy disappeared.

Every now and then, you'd hear a rumour about his next fight. The M-1 team were keen to use him as a substitute one time but it never happened. It wasn't as though he got beaten up by a mug. Carwin was the name on everyone's lips. He went from strength to strength. Wainy had landed early. A little more belief, a little more power and he could have had him over. In the talent vacuum that is the Heavyweight division; that would guarantee a couple more pay cheques and would generate title shot talk. Instead, he was cut loose.

Neil Wain resurfaced at the ZT Fight Night, 16 months after UFC 89. How could he resist? Ten grand on the table for an eight man tournament for British heavies; winner takes all. Neil got the toughest draw; Rob 'The Bear' Broughton. Neil did well. Showed he'd been working hard at his game. Showed he was better than all the two bob mugs with blogs gave him credit for. The growing number of Brit's on the UFC roster was drawing a backlash from American writers. Wainy's 90 second beating coupled with his flabby physique made him a target for mockery. His name had become shorthand for the inadequacy of British fighters. Neil did well, but not quite well enough. Rob caught him in a guillotine in the second round and went on to win the tournament. That was enough to convince the powers that be that he was ready to step up to the UFC. He was the next Brit to get a golden ticket and the dream of making a decent living.

Where it stops nobody knows...

EXILE ON MAIN STREET

- Have you had a good time?

- I have actually. I've been quite surprised with myself. It got very absorbing. Interestingly, the more violent it got, the more absorbing it got.

When I fell into writing about MMA, one person I didn't expect to end up interviewing was the debonair former Cabinet Minister Michael Portillo. Since his days of Thatcherite excess, Portillo has reinvented himself as a media personality and has become that rarest of commodities; a popular Tory. It was easy to see how he'd pulled it off. He came over as thoroughly decent chap; open, polite and fair minded. I was talking to him after he'd witnessed the Jim Wallhead/Fabricio Nascimento fight. The Portillo verdict:

- That was an amazing bout. It went the distance. It was quite finely balanced. It had a lot of aggression; a lot of to and fro.'

Michael was up in Nottingham on business not pleasure. He was making a documentary for the BBC Science strand Horizon. The premise of the film was that he felt he had no violence in him whatsoever (a bit of a weird statement for a former Defence Secretary to make I thought, but I let it go) and he was testing this belief. As it turned out, the Cage Warriors show ended up being a few short clips in the finished programme. Portillo returned to his frankly creepy couch bound relationship with Diane Abbott and, despite being outspoken on the issues of the day, he has never once mentioned the injustices suffered by his favourite fighter Jimmy Wallhead on This Week. That is the way with UK MMA. It is suitable fare for documentaries and tabloid scare stories about the cage fighting menace and that's about it. For all the conviction that Mixed Martial Arts is going to be the next big thing, mainstream acceptance is still a distant hope.

Another question I asked Michael Portillo, and one that he deftly sidestepped, was about his stance on the local councils who effectively banned MMA in their areas. Like boxing, house music and most other things worth bothering with- MMA had not been initially welcomed by those with authority. Although there has been no legislation to counter the menace in the UK, as there was with those pesky cheesy quavers and their repetitive beats,

MMA has been banned at the back door in some areas. Local councillors live for the chance of a cheap headline. Local bureaucrats live to avoid risk or nuisance at all costs. These two interests come together and form a coalition against the cage fighting peril.

A classic example was the blow out of Cage Warriors: Showdown 3 in early 2007. The show was all set for Wolverhampton Civic Hall when the council pulled the plug. A spokesperson said that the council had found that the event was not suitable for their venue. What they meant by this is unclear. In the previous 12 months, the Civic had hosted James McSweeney's head kick KO and a Babyshambles gig. Seemingly, a band fronted by Britain's most famous junkie Pete Doherty; best known for jacking up unconscious groupies, his nihilistic anthem 'Fuck Forever' and wearing a hat with a hole in it is acceptable entertainment for the Wolves youth, but a combat sports event pitching top class athletes against each other is not. Rebellious rock n roll bands on a scuzzy tip are something we are used to and accept. Mixed Martial Arts is a sport which is not yet fully understood by the general public.

Misinformation, confusion and, it has to be said, some questionable marketing mean that it has not been embraced by many as a genuine sport. Until it is- MMA will remain in the sights of grandstanding politicians and nervy health and safety obsessed civil servants.

Some opponents really should know better. Most press articles attacking the sport contain a quote from a boxing guy; some arrangement of the words brutal, animals and uncivilised. They conveniently forget the outlaw past of the prize ring.

In days of yore, prizefighting was an underground activity. Like ravers and football hoolies, the fancy would get wind of a fight through the grapevine then assemble miles from the grasp of the authorities. The language of these early contests, where a challenger would throw his hat into the ring and a fighter would prove he could continue by coming up to scratch, is with us to this day.

Gradually, the noble art of bruising became a respectable pursuit and provided a new set of idioms for the masses: saved by the bell, on the ropes, throw in the towel, the gloves are off, come out fighting, blow by blow account, ringside seat, sparring partner, seconds out, punch drunk, below the belt, down and out, taking a dive, roll with the punches, in-fighting, a good man to have in your corner, pull your punches, ring rusty, bobbing and weaving, beat him to the punch, out for the count, on his toes and the deadly knockout blow. Every titanic encounter in sport, politics or showbiz borrows the metaphor of two Heavyweights slugging it out in the final round. Forget sport, no other activity has contributed as much to modern English as pugilism. Boxing was more than a sport. It was all life's struggles and triumphs distilled into three minute rounds, with a supporting cast of villains, saints and cheats. The drama inherent in fight sports meant that boxing seeped into the common psyche.

Leading boxers crossed over to become national institutions.

The glory days are long gone. From the highpoint of Benn and Eubank live on prime time ITV, the decline has been rapid. A variety of factors can be blamed, but they are basically different shades of greed.

Some members of the boxing fraternity have now identified MMA as another threat to their dwindling empire. As well as the bad mouthing, there are rumours of boxing promoters having a word with venue owners and TV execs in an attempt to stifle their upstart competitor. A risky strategy indeed: telling councillors that MMA is a bit more brutal than their sport and telling TV people not to cover something because it's popular with the kids. Touchy local councils still shut down the odd show, but the tide appears to be turning. In these cash strapped times, a quid is a quid. Conversely, convincing TV companies to invest the funds required for a live outside broadcast is a bigger ask than ever.

If I had a pound for every time I'd written an article that described MMA as: 'the first new sport of the internet age'... I'd have about a fiver. The rapid growth of the sport, particularly in the USA has led to some bold statements. Zuffa President Dana White has predicted that the UFC will become bigger than soccer worldwide. His vision is world domination; a future where phrases like tap or snap, passing the guard and flattened out with the hooks in enter the vernacular. Dana flags up an innate human appreciation of appreciation of fighting. He famously said that if there is a baseball game on one corner, a basketball game on another, a hockey game on another and a fight breaks out on a fourth- the crowd will all naturally gravitate to the fight. I'd agree with that, but you could also argue that if a bloke dressed up as a clown was shagging a goat on the corner, a mixture of curiosity and disgust would also attract any passing trade.

The MMA explosion can be best understood by looking at the other smash hits of the internet age. In 1994, seven months after UFC 1, ESPN televised the Extreme Games, the forerunner of the X Games; a festival of skateboarding, biking and street sports. Three years later the hot dog-tastic Winter X Games followed and a few ways of attempted suicide in the ocean were added the summer version. In 1992 Professional Bull Riders Inc was formed in an attempt to revitalise the sport of bull riding. The PBR tour broke out of traditional rodeo country to pack out arenas around North America. How far has bull riding come? They have converted so many city slickers they can sell a three night stand at Madison Square Garden. Yee Har. Another activity that harks back to the Wild West is poker. Movies have told me that cowboys liked nothing better than a few hands down the saloon after a hard day on the range. Poker has become a surprise TV hit and a multibillion dollar, internet fuelled industry.

All of the recent boom sports are celebrations of individualism. Pre-industrial societies put champions of their wrestling and horse racing festivals on a pedestal. Prizefighting only beats horse racing by a nose in terms of influence on the English language. When the masses headed to the cities, social relations changed and leisure activities mirrored this. Man was no longer an island; co-operation was needed to achieve things at work and at play. The upper and middle classes played Cricket and Rugby Union. Games that reflected the social order they upheld. Games where the captain was the key figure who dictated tactics to subordinates- each of whom had a strictly defined role. The working class embraced sports where a collective functioned in order for each member to have the opportunity to express themselves. Rugby League broke away from the shackles of its toffee nosed masters and developed into a free flowing celebration of athleticism and skill. Football conquered the world- except for the US; a rigidly hierarchical society that has a version of football that clings to master and servant relations on the field. The late, great Liverpool manager Bill Shankly described football played the right way as 'socialism without the politics' and he was on the money.

The rise of MMA, along with poker and the extreme sports, has come in an era when the old certainties of life and work have fallen apart. The traditional industries with their unions and close communities are all but dead. The forces of capitalism, with a helping hand from the

BLOODY REVOLUTION

Thatcher/Reagan axis, have changed the face of the Western world. Mrs T said there is no such thing as society. Her children have been brought up to believe that it's a dog eat dog world. When the chips are down- you have to rely on yourself. The welfare state is going, the next generation is going to be poorer than its parents: you are on your own in a hostile environment. Welcome to the Wild Western World. Stress and insecurity push people to extremes. How are you going to get your kicks? Online Texas hold em? Risking your stack in the hope of proving you're The Man. At the end of the day, this kind of virtual confrontation, like all sporting contests, is a substitute for fighting. Why not try the real thing? Get down to your local gym and learn how to take people down literally. At the end of the day, these are real life skills that are going to be more useful to you in a hairy situation than skateboarding ever will (unless you are friendly with a wacky scientist and accidentally get transported back to 1955). As we search for heroes in this age of uncertainty, surely we're going to look to the individuals are best equipped to look after themselves. The ultimate fighters.

At the moment, for all the advances in the last decade, MMA fans exist in a ghetto. There are parallels with other subcultures. Surfers support a sport that has health benefits and an element of danger. Surfing has also spawned a variety of fashion and lifestyle brands that are worn by non participants who want to show they share the spirit of the board riders.

There are also divisions in the ranks of MMA fans. All tend to have a certain indie band elitism that sets them apart from ordinary people. There are certain articles of faith like: Pride ruled and anyone who doesn't get grappling is an idiot. Other than that- you can roughly split UK fans in the way that you can categorize football fans. The vast majority are strictly UFC fans. This group are the equivalent of Premier League fans. They are big on personalities and merchandise, have never seen a live show and tend to know absolutely zilch about the sport beyond the Octagon. The people who turn up to the shows promoted by domestic organisations are like lower division fans. Many have some kind of bond with the fighters they are turning out to watch and plenty have actual experience of martial arts training. They follow the big boys but prefer the up close excitement of small hall action. For the price of a crow's nest seat at a UFC event, you can be close enough to get warm blood in your pint at a local show. MMA also has a layer of fans similar to the football nerds who read When Saturday Comes and bore people about Eredivisie games they've seen on ESPN. The fight version worship at the shrine of Japanese MMA and find a work day morning huddled over a laptop more enjoyable than a few cageside jars with the lads.

Advances in technology have made this kind of fandom possible. Very little MMA exists that can't be tracked down by anyone with OK computer skills. Some enterprising blighters have produced shows specifically to feed the appetite of the hardcore MMA fan. A few years ago, Rio Heroes was launched on internet pay per view. From what looked like a cellar in Brazil, bare knuckle, no holds barred fights were streamed on the net. Low level fighters beating the shit out of each other for the benefit of grubby people. That's progress. Was I watching? Of course I was, and I would have stubbed a Benson out on Debbie Harry's tit if she'd been close by.

When it comes to media coverage, MMA is truly a sport of the internet age. In the early days, this came out of necessity. No established media outlet would touch this renegade freakshow with a barge pole. Fortunately, the World Wide Web was spreading. Enthusiasts set up their own websites and blogs to get the word out. Years down the line, some of these fan generated sites have gone on to become the new establishment. In true indie kid style, fans will mercilessly slag off anyone who they decide is: out of touch, elitist or (shock horror) only in it for the money.

Also mirroring the punk rock, D.I.Y., ethic; anyone can set up their own blog or put out a podcast with a potential audience beyond the imagination of any megalomaniac 80s media baron. This is fantastic as it enables us to hear the voices of great writers and broadcasters who would never have had a chance in the past. This is also terrible as the absence of entry requirements, professional standards and ethics mean you have to wade through so much shit to get to the good stuff. Few blogs produce original content. Instead, they exist in an echo chamber, where a story breaks and, one by one, the blog masters give their take on the matter.

Some of the pioneers have come from humble beginnings to become substantial concerns; loved and loathed in equal measure. Sherdog.com, once the hobby of a chunky Californian photographer is now a multi media extravaganza, pumping out hours of original radio content each day alongside its written news and comment. The thing is; we ain't seen nothing yet.

I interviewed a couple of the leading lights of Sherdog. TJ DeSantis runs the radio output from a garage in Minnesota. The shows he produces reach hundreds of thousands across the globe but this may just be the tip of the iceberg. Once technology takes a couple more baby steps, the world will truly be his oyster. As he told me:

- You can't be driving around in your car and say: 'I want to listen the new Sherdog Radio Network podcast' and be able to download it to your car. You have to go home. You have to set aside some time to download it. I think eventually, your in car stereo will have wi –fi. It will be able to log onto the internet and download that show for you. Podcasts are going to be around forever. The AM and FM dial is dying. When people want to listen to a song, they turn on their iPod. Why sit there and listen to what the radio wants me to when I can make a play list and be away?

BLOODY REVOLUTION

For the same piece, I talked to Jordan Breen, the Mark Kermode of MMA radio. He's been a beneficiary of internet democracy, but is well aware of its drawbacks.

- As something becomes easier for people to do, it means that people who are less qualified to do it do it. Everyone has the ability to speak their mind, but a lot of people's minds are full of horrific, awful, vitriolic, racist, nationalistic, retarded inane backward bullshit. Before, opinions were made by newspapers and the people who read the news and there was a vetting process. You had to be a relatively intelligent person. You couldn't start your own pirate radio station and take over the universe with retarded opinions. The internet enables in the most fantastic ways and it also enables in the most miserable and awful of ways.

Breen was talking about podcasting, but his words are a perfect summing up of that other mighty pillar of the MMA world; the internet forum. Facebook, Twitter and whatever new social networking sensation has taken over by the time you read this; they are all well and good, but it is the forum that has been at the centre of MMA on the net. Forums are places where fans, fighters and promoters can interact with each other- usually dragging each other down to cesspool level. Sherdog has one of the biggest forums with some of the most brainless posters. A few years ago, someone told me that there was a long thread on there about one of my magazine articles. Feeling very smug, I checked it out and saw that my piece had inspired over 500 comments. By the time I had finished reading them, I had a bleaker world view. Only one person had actually read the article and the other posts showed the intellectual rigour of a three you old girl throwing mash potato at someone then sticking her fingers in her ears and blowing a raspberry.

The daddy of the forums is The Underground at mixedmartialarts.com. In the UK, we have the infamous cagewarriors.com. For a few years, cagewarriors has been the place that the UK MMA community gathers to discuss the issues of the day. Periodically, some of the bigger names desert the forum on the reasonable grounds that they are sick of being insulted by morons, but it remains essential reading for anyone with a connection to the business. Populated by wits, experts, trolls, pondlife and borderline psychopaths, its biggest selling point is the fact that industry insiders often use the forum to attack their competitors. Sometimes this is done slyly with finesse; often it is name calling and threats.

The room for error in our technology rich, intelligence poor times was highlighted by the Kimo affair. Kimo Leopoldo was a star of the early UFCs, mainly due to his gimmick of carrying a cross to the cage in the Jesus style. On a July morning in 2009, someone posted the details of Kimo's death on The Underground. Apparently, he had suffered a heart attack in Costa Rica. The blogs went into overdrive, many of them speculating that Kimo had died as a result of steroid abuse; others labelled him a meth addict. The celebrity website TMZ ran the story and was followed by a number of reputable newspapers. As it turned out, Kimo was not dead- he was just tired. He slept through the whole thing, only finding out when he checked his cellphone and found it jammed with hundreds of messages. All were along the lines of: 'Hi Kimo. Is it true that you're dead?'

Not checking the facts, style over substance, so called writers who use 'of' as a verb- these are not MMA problems. These things are part of the irresistible new media takeover. No more Morecambe and Wise Christmas Show with 25 million viewers. No more household names. As the media becomes more fragmented and more specialised, the idea of the shared televised experience will seem as archaic as the penny farthing. Even what we are sold as the great unifying sporting events, like England's World Cup matches, draw a fraction of what they did a couple of decades ago. At the moment, for all the hype, there are still a lot of people in the UK who have never heard of MMA and a larger group who have a vague image of it being some sort of cross between Gladiators and prison rape. There is room for the sport to develop and prosper, but those who chase the mainstream audience are doomed to failure. There is no mainstream anymore.

Yet still they chase.

TOM 'KONG' WATSON
V
ALEX REID

THE FIGHT OF OUR LIVES

ACT I

Throughout history, poetic souls have used fights and fighters to evoke the spirit of an age. Jack Dempsey was the Roaring Twenties; a brash brawler who was going to grab everything he could on his terms. After riding the rods from doss house to hobo camp, the Manassa Mauler became the embodiment of the American Dream as he rose up to become the Heavyweight champion of the world. He even had the chutzpah to park his belt for three years while he headed to Hollywood to chase movie stardom.

Joe Louis was the perfect, understated hero for the depressed 30s. By the end of the decade, America was being woken from isolationism and forced to accept its role as an international superpower. In June 1938, Louis confronted Max Schmeling, the poster boy of Nazi Germany. Joe destroyed Schmeling in two minutes- inspiring the 70,000 packed into Yankee Stadium and millions across the nation.

The struggle for civil rights, the rise of youth, the cultural revolution that rocked the old order- Ali personi- fied the 1960s. He was the loudmouthed kid who shook up the world. After his three year exile for refusing to serve in Vietnam, Ali came back ready to reclaim his title in the Fight of the Century at Madison Square Garden. Frazier messed up his Ali's face, floored him with a left hook in the 15th and took a unanimous decision.

The Sixties were over. Ali rose again, but it was never the same. In his second spell at the top, he didn't dance and he wasn't pretty. They say that if you can you remember the Sixties, you weren't really there. Ali's absent mindedness is a hangover from the headshots he ate in his rope a dope years. A love child casualty who stuck around at the party after the flowers had started dying.

Mike Tyson was the last champion. Invincible and insatiable. The markets boomed on the back of the laissez faire policies of the time and Western capitalism was an unstoppable force. Tyson became unbearably human in the tenth round against Buster Douglas in Tokyo. He bit the canvas and the world around him caved in. The smoke and mirrors that had elevated supply side economics to commandment footing cracked. The Eighties boom was built on the sand of unsecured credit and junk bonds. The ugly heart that had fuelled the excess was exposed. Tyson went to jail for taking the doctrine of self gratification uber alles to its logical conclusion.

If you want to understand what the 20th century was about, don't read a worthy history book. Close your eyes and listen to the version of the Star Spangled Banner that Jimi Hendrix performed at Woodstock; a guttural take on a classic theme. The high handed notions of nationalism, egotism and moral superiority undercut by the down and dirty forces necessary to uphold them. A fairytale supported by invisible monsters.

References can be more specific. The United Kingdom in the early 21st century is a confused place. Nobody believes in anything. Style trumps substance in every area of life. We are ruled by a coalition of spin doctors and advertising executives. Our cultural life is dominated by the celebrity whirl. Achieving excellence or discovering truth and beauty: strictly for losers. A whole generation motivated by the desire to be on telly: look at me, look at me. An infantile disorder presented as a high ideal in a post imperialist nation still trying to come to terms with its reduced circumstances.

If you want to understand the United Kingdom in the early 21st century- watch Tom 'Kong' Watson v Alex Reid.

BLOODY REVOLUTION

The fight was announced in November 2009. On May 15th 2010, the pair were going to go at it in the main event of BAMMA 3 at the LG Arena in Birmingham. Oh yeah, BAMMA were back and they had a plan. They were banking on the celebrity of the best known cage fighter in history to bring in the casual viewers who had not yet enjoyed the MMA experience. In the lead up, there was going to be a TV series to build interest and the big fight was going to be aired live on Bravo.

Alex Reid is the most famous UK MMA fighter by a distance. He also is one of the true pioneers of the scene, starting out in the 90s when promoters were literally making up the rules as they went along. In one of his early fights, he defeated the man who preceded him as the holder of the Britain's most famous cage fighter title. Lightning Lee Murray went on to compete in the UFC, but that doesn't get you a great deal of attention in the UK. He shot to fame when he was named as the mastermind of the Securitas depot heist. Clocking in at £53 million, it was the biggest cash robbery in British history and Murray is currently serving time in Morocco on charges relating to it. Lee was number one with a bullet before Reidy broke big.

Away from the cage, Alex attended a course at the Guildford School of Acting and went on to land a role in Channel 4's pre-teen masturbatory aid Hollyoaks. Cage Rage would always bill Alex as a full blown soap star. Sneering internet critics have dismissed him as a glorified extra. As no-one on Earth admits they have ever seen the show, the size of his contribution looks set to remain a mystery. Some other graduates of the Mersey soap have since gone on to become staples of the reality TV circuit but most fade into obscurity.

Alex returned to his first love- fighting. He was known as a kickboxer and compiled a solid MMA record. Even in his rare defeats, such as his loss to Mark Weir, he enhanced his reputation by showing true grit. The numbers on his CV took a dip when he became a regular on Cage Rage. His record at Wembley was 2-6-1 (The solitary draw coming courtesy of very kind judging after he was dominated on the ground by Daijiro Matsui). The truth is, he was ridiculously overmatched. A good, honest pro who was being put in against guys with genuine international class.

Alex was characterised as someone who wanted to test himself against the best. Unfortunately, the test results were always negative. He seemed to be trying too hard; from the forced smile to the too tight shorts. His efforts bought plenty of goodwill, but interest in his career was dwindling.

Controversy followed Alex around, even in the early days. His 1999 fight against Lee Murray ended in confusion. Murray's corner men were unhappy about Reid's illegal use of the ropes during the fight and violent scenes marred the event at the Epping Forest Country Club.

BLOODY REVOLUTION

At a Millennium Brawl show, Alex constantly grabbed the cage to avoid being taken down by Jean Silva. He was disqualified in the third round, but the result was changed to a no contest later.

Next up was another noted grappler, Matt Ewin. Reid won in the opening round, but found himself in another shit storm. Ewin accused him of greasing- a dastardly trick employed by stand up fighters who wish to avoid being taken down to the mat. You make yourself slimy and hard to keep hold of by applying oils to yourself. To evade detection, slippery customers can rub the grease deep into the skin and then take a shower. After passing the pre-fight checks from the ref, they start to sweat out their own protective layer as soon as the action commences. Years later, when they were rematched on a Cage Rage card, Reid presented Ewin with a bottle of baby oil at the weigh in.

In the early stages of his fight with up and coming French kickboxer Xavier 'Professor X' Foupa Pokam, Alex had to retire due to an eye poke. Against 'Ninja' Rua, he was forced out with a bizarre cut to the shin that started gushing claret after less than thirty seconds. Reid couldn't buy a win and it was hard to see a future for him in the sport. UK MMA had moved on and Alex Reid looked like one of yesterday's men.

The side projects weren't working out either. Alex was chosen to front a set of training documentaries in which he visited top gyms around the world. It was one of those many schemes bodged together by media folk who think they've finally come up with a way to get people to pay to look at stuff on the internet. It went the same way as all the similar brilliant ideas. The quest for fame looked over. Alex was known as a 'character' in the same way a bloke with a loud shirt and a line in old gags down the pub is. You smile at him, but really you wish he'd just go away.

Alex was thrown a lifeline when he made it to the final selection stage for a place on the ninth season of The Ultimate Fighter. He was one of the sixteen who travelled to the Wolfslair gym. Each had one fight; winner gets a ticket to Vegas. Loser goes home.

Alex was drawn against Dean Amasinger, a Rough House product who had still been a schoolboy when Alex set out on his pro career. The fights took place without an audience, except for UFC President Dana White, Team UK coach Michael Bisping and the rivals for the Team USA coaching spot: Dan Henderson and Rich Franklin. As always, Alex makes an effort to stand out. He enters with his arms aloft.

- Alright. Reidernator time.

Bisping shouts good luck. He's served his time on the harsh coal face of the UK scene. He knows it is Reid's last shot and wishes the veteran well.

In the cage, Alex mugs for the camera. In his pre-fight interview, he had talked about how he didn't need to get aggressive or angry. He would look into his opponent's eyes and see his soul. The words sounded over rehearsed. Laboured and unconvincing, like the work of a bad actor.

- WOO. Come on baby.

Behind the bravado, there is an aura of desperation.

In the fight, Dean is in charge on the feet, traditionally the strongest part of Reid's game. Dean then picks Alex up and dumps him to the canvas like a sack of spuds. As he works from the top, Alex catches him in a triangle choke. The ringside jury are convinced that the fight is over. Reidy is going to Vegas; TV time and the chance to show his star quality. All he's ever wanted. It slips away. Dana White can't believe his eyes.

- How the fuck did he get out of that? He had it full.

Dean takes the initiative. He punches his grounded opponent. Alex runs his mouth.

- Come on Dean. Hit me. Is that it?

Bisping offers some well thought out analysis.

- He needs to get back to his feet and stop going WOO.

The fight ends. Reid raises his arms.

-WOO. One more round.

The judges agree. TUF bouts are two rounds long. If the judges have the scores even, they go to a third, 'sudden victory' round; what would be called sudden death in any sport where there is no chance of a sudden death actually occurring. Dean continues to beat Alex at his own game. The Reid corner appeal to him.

- Stop showboating.

It looks like he doesn't have the gas to mount any kind of meaningful attack and is content to brazen out the round.

The fight goes to the ground and Dean almost manages to snatch defeat from the jaws of victory when he falls into the Reid triangle again. At the end, Alex puts his arms up triumphantly. He defiantly shouts 'yeah' as he waits for the decision, but no one is buying the act. Referee Goddard raises Dean's hand. The dream is over. Nothing up their sleeves. No magic, little Alex.

A few months later, Alex Reid was a household name. His new found fame had nothing to do with fighting. Alex was invited out by Sol Gilbert, a former Cage Rage stalwart who had established the ZT Fitness and personal training brand on the South Coast. Sol was meeting up with one of his clients and thought Alex might like to tag along. Alex and the client hit it off and soon became an item. The client in question was called Katie Price.

It is difficult to try and explain the Katie Price phenomenon to anyone who has been brought up outside to the UK. Even for us Brits, it's still a little perplexing. Katie started out as a glamour model- going by the name of Jordan. She first appeared on page 3 in 1996 and soon established herself in the front rank of tits out talent. You can count the number of models who have gone on to have successful media careers on the fingers of a leper's hand, but Jordan went from strength to strength. Her two big selling points (stop tittering at the back) were her penchant for plastic surgery and her 'private' life. Jordan kept getting bigger, especially in the breast department. Katie created an outrageous character, leaving her natural look behind by jacking up the implants and putting on her slap with a trowel. Her love life became a soap opera, played out in the gossip columns with walk ons from a Gladiator, Teddy Sheringham and spiky topped, stuttering virgin Gareth Gates. Her relationship with boyband star Dane Bowers melted in the spotlight and the gory details gripped many of the sadder members of our society.

In 2002, Jordan had a baby. The father was Manchester United striker Dwight Yorke. Motherhood broadened her appeal as she was featured in magazines discussing the trials and tribulations of bringing up a child as a single parent.

She was doing well, but her fame level went off the charts in 2004 when she appeared on the third series of the ITV reality show; I'm a Celebrity...Get Me Out of Here!. Jordan was stranded in the jungle with Sex Pistols' front man John Lydon, chicken nugget queen Kerry Katona and a bunch of C-listers. Desperately fighting relegation to the Z-list was former teenybop heart throb Peter Andre.

Jordan and Peter were perfect for each other. She was a single minded operator who liked everything to march to her beat. He was a nice bloke who came over as a bit dim. They met on camera and went on to live on camera. Their courtship, marriage, family life and eventual break up were all filmed and packaged as reality shows for ITV 2. The mundane lives of dull people repackaged as aspirational fodder for the masses. It could almost be ITV 2's slogan. The whole channel resembles a recruiting video for Al Qaeda. If a society can find the time to watch Judge Judy or repeats of Airline- surely it deserves to fall.

The rise of Katie Price continued apace. She and Andre got his and hers ITV 2 shows after their split and the public lapped up the bad blood as the estranged couple took digs at each other. Katie was a fag hag's dream woman; high hems, big hair and Krusty cosmetics. Within a certain demographic, she is looked up to as a role model. Four volumes of her autobiography have been best sellers, as have a number of racy novels with her name on them. Her brand also sells products ranging from lingerie to riding tack. Every day, the red tops carry a story about Katie. The Daily Star manages to manufacture a front page splash about her most days. The Mail and Express regularly print snooty articles that look down on the Price lifestyle, but always make sure they decorate it with a few shots of her enhanced cleavage for the moralistic Middle Englanders to have a good perve at. She owns her own production company and her wealth is estimated at £40 million.

Katie Price is arguably the most famous woman in Britain. She is certainly the most photographed. For better or worse- she is a symbol of what the nation has become. When he was seen with her, Alex Reid became a player in a news item. When he was identified as her new squeeze (JORDAN GRAPPLES CAGE FIGHTER), he became newsworthy in his own right. Every day, he would pop up in the paper as unnamed sources close to Katie and Peter would discuss his role in the pair's rush to the divorce courts. Alex- he just looked happy to be there.

As far as fighting went, Alex was limiting himself to contests under UK-1 rules; basically kickboxing in a cage. After the TUF letdown, he returned to the fray at Ultimate Challenge in February 2009 and took the UK-1 title on points. Shortly before he became Jordan's plus one, he defended his belt.

Nineteen year old Jake Bostwick came out swinging for the fences. Reid used his head, bided his time then dropped the boy with a knee to the chin. The Reidernator was back on song. The acclaim lasted for approximately 20 seconds. That was about the time it took for Alex to think it would be a good idea to walk over to Bostwick, place his foot on the grounded body of his still dazed adversary and pose as the conquering hero. Although he apologised, Alex lost a lot of goodwill with his antics that night.

Katie turned up to support her man when he defended his title against Jack Mason at Ultimate Challenge: Mayhem in September 2009. From being a crowd favour-ite, Reid was now cast as the villain of the piece- his name booed whenever it was mentioned. He scraped home, taking a razor thin decision, further angering the crowd.

At that point, Katie Price was invited into the cage. Naturally she got booed and responded in kind. Shouting variations on theme of 'fuck you', Katie gave the mob the two fingered salute.

All the national papers had a man on site and they wrote up descriptions of the unedifying spectacle.

The night was also the focus of an episode of Price's fly on the wall show; 'What Katie Did Next'. Obviously, this version of events was edited to show Alex and particularly Katie in the best possible light. The joy of reality TV is that it can portray whichever specific reality the producer wants the public to see.

BAMMA added two and two and thought the answer was big bucks. Mixed Martial Arts was the fastest growing sport in the world. Alex Reid was the subject of huge press attention because he was dating a national icon. If you put together a big MMA event headlined by Alex Reid, you could attract a new wave of casual fans to the sport. That brain storming session must have been a beauty. They decided to throw the kitchen sink at it. Why not produce a series starring Alex Reid to get maximum attention in the run up to the event? A celebrity, the fastest growing sport in the world and reality TV- the golden triangle. Throw in the whiff of sex lingering in the background and you have a sure fire ratings smash.

BLOODY REVOLUTION

All they needed now was the right opponent. Someone with charisma who would come across well on TV. Someone who had credibility in the sport. Ideally, someone who would be prepared to stand up and play Reidy at his own game. Tom 'Kong' Watson fitted the bill.

All hardcore fight fans pretend to hate flamboyant ring walks. We'd rather cut to the action. That's what we say anyway, but we get caught up in it all the same as anyone else. In UK MMA, we haven't got anyone who crosses the line to showbiz as far as a Genki Sudo, a Sakuraba or a Prince Naseem. We've got Tom Watson.

'Kong' was on the same Cage Rage bill as the McSweeney/Paczkow scrap. He was up against house fighter Mark 'The Beast' Epstein. From the speakers, a soft voice told a long, dull nursery story about a beast terrorising a village. The pay off was something convoluted about someone beautiful slaying the beast to make the people happy.

After this protracted set up, the theme tune from Beauty and the Beast kicked in. Tom Watson entered the arena wearing his usual gorilla mask, plus added accessories in the form of the kind of hat and flowing dress which would be worn by a damsel in distress. I'm all for showmanship, but this was dangerously naff. Then I noticed that the red faced Cockney wretch next to me was disgusted. With all the bile he could muster, fat boy yelled:

- You facking gorilla puff.

From that moment, I was a Kong fan for life.

Epstein controlled Tom on the ground to win on points. Watson had come to the sport from a stand up background, but he was doing his best to catch up. He'd joined the exodus to New Mexico to learn at the knee of Greg Jackson. Tom respected the sport. He lived the life and dedicated himself to self improvement.

After the Epstein setback, he went on to clock up two more wins at Cage Rage; one of them a spectacular upkick KO of Pierre Guillet.

Tom became the first Ultimate Challenge Middleweight champion when he defeated Daniel Cubitt. He had been due to meet Matt Ewin, who was on a four fight winning streak including revenge over Reid, but Ewin had to pull out. The contrast between Watson and the late replacement was obvious during the build up on the big screens. Tom talked about his rigorous preparations at the camp many rate as the world's best. Daniel admitted he was quite new to this MMA lark. The fight went as you'd expect. Tom took the lad apart- knocking him out with a knee to the head in less than two minutes. Kong marched on to the first BAMMA show in June 2009, once again showcasing his striking to stop John Maguire.

People were sitting up and taking notice. There was the usual talk about the big shows coming in. Tom had the connections from his time spent across the Atlantic. In his win over the heavy handed John Philips, he'd shown brains and a functional ground game. Tom Watson was far from the finished article, but he had more going for him than some guys who'd got the call.

Alex Reid v Tom Watson was announced in early November 2009. By this time, Reidy was a fixture in the media. The juiciest stories were a supposed feud between himself and Peter Andre, a twisted quote about a possible fight with Joe Calzaghe and the revelation that Alex was a cross dresser with an alter ego called Roxanne.

In general, Alex got a bad press. Knocking Jordan was a national pastime and he was not as savvy as her in his dealings with the papers. MMA got a lot more column inches in the press, mainly shock horror pieces about the brutal nature of the world that Jordan's feller was involved in.

Alex took stick from what you could loosely describe as the MMA community. The weirdest piece of journalism concerned a post on cagewarriors.com. A member of the forum made a ludicrously over the top threat, saying he would slash one of Jordan's horses and the News of the World decided to make a salacious news story out of a pathetic piece of forum trolling.

Among non psychopathic fans, there was little enthusiasm for the fight. The old maxim 'there's no such thing as bad publicity' has a ring of truth, but each time the Jordan circus had come into contact with the UK MMA scene, it had generated nothing but bad vibes.

In sporting terms, it made no sense for a rising star to fight a guy who had lost his last six MMA bouts. The fight game thrives on controversy, but this bout came with a built in sleaze factor. What would be the cost of bringing the sport to a wider audience? The spotlight would be shone on a mismatch with the attendance of the lady at the top the Heat generation's most hated list as the real main attraction.

At the back end of 2009, Alex Reid was in the news again. Katie Price returned to I'm a Celebrity...Get Me Out of Here!, reportedly picking up £350,000 for her trouble. The great British public voted in huge numbers to ensure she had to take every single challenge on offer. After almost drowning, being covered in thousands of cockroaches and being forced to eat a kangaroo's anus, Price decided enough was enough and walked out. The papers had all reported that Alex had headed out to Australia and was going to propose to her. What was Katie's first act when she left the jungle? She dumped Alex Reid live on prime time ITV. Even though the couple were soon back together, the incident shaped the public's perception of Alex Reid. It also showed the fragility of his fame. He needed to do something to prove he was some-thing more than Jordan's boy toy.

Three days into the New Year, Alex Reid entered the Celebrity Big Brother House to a chorus of boos. If the angry mob had had a kangaroo's anus on them, they would have force fed it to him.

Big Brother had become a national obsession- the daddy of all reality TV. The normal version had enjoyed massive support from the press who were delighted to have something to fill their papers with in the silly season when parliament was not in session, the football season was over and everyone had buggered off on holiday. The show produced a new kind of famous person- naïve and eager to please, unlike the hardened, PR protected celebrities. Although Alex was classed as a real celebrity, he came over much more like the fame hungry wannabes who fill the regular show.

The rest of the line up ranged from the internationally famous (Ivana Trump) to footnotes in trash history (Nicola T). Alex had plenty in common with other housemates, notably Katyia (famous for shagging a famous person), Dane Bowers (former boyfriend of Jordan) and Vinnie Jones (shit actor. In an edition of Big Brother's Big Mouth, host Davina McCall had to keep telling the audience that a clip from Reid's movie Killer Bitch was genuine as they howled with laughter at the impossibly wooden acting).

Life in the house did not start well for Alex. As usual, he seemed to be trying too hard to be liked. Actor and Christian bore Stephen Baldwin took him under his wing and began schooling little Alex in the ways of the big book.

More worryingly for BAMMA, he started to give Alex career advice. Baldwin told him that he should forget about fighting. With his raised profile after Big Brother, the world would be his oyster. He should forget any measly fight contract and make hay while the sun was shining. Alex could see he was talking sense.

In a situation like Big Brother, it is impossible to hide your true character. The pressure and constant surveillance mean that the real you will come out no matter how hard you try to hide behind a front. Alex Reid was exposed for what he really is: a nice bloke. After 27 days, he emerged from the house to be greeted by a cheering crowd. Alex Reid had won the popular vote and was crowned the winner. Straight after, he jetted off to marry Katie Price in Las Vegas. Alex Reid was finally famous.

Meanwhile, Tom Watson was keeping busy. He fought the Canadian Travis Galbraith on a Maximum Fighting Championship card in Edmonton, Alberta. This was a step up. Galbraith had been around the block on name North American promotions for years and won more than he lost. 'Kong' showed solid takedown defence in the clinch then knocked the veteran out cold with a magnificent head kick. Galbraith fell face first like he'd been shot in the back of the head: an image of exquisite ferocity. Within minutes, the footage was winging its way round the wired world. Tom had sent out a message and it had been received loud and clear.

Whenever I was at an event, the talk would turn to the fight. The UK MMA scene was taking the Baldwin line. Nobody believed it was going to happen. It was a backward step for Tom and there seemed to be even less upside for Alex. If he went ahead with the fight, he would lose. He may well lose badly. He was hot and needed to get out there and exploit his fame while the media were still interested in him. Locking himself away in a proper training camp and letting the buzz die down seemed nuts. Even if Alex pulled off a shock win- what good did it do him? Every fighter is always struggling to climb the ladder to the big international shows. The likes of the UFC wouldn't give Alex a second glance. He was in his mid thirties and past his best. He was on his way out so why not get out now. He could earn more from doing easy celeb nonsense than the guys fighting on the big shows did anyway. If he got humiliated: it would hurt his image and his earning potential. He had to pull out.

Soon after Celebrity Big Brother, pictures of Alex without Katie started to appear in the papers. He was off filming his show that was to build up to his fight at BAMMA 3. The premise of the series was that Alex would travel the world to seek new different techniques to use against Tom. After studying a new martial art each week, he would engage in a challenge. If that sounds like a low grade knock off of Human Weapon or Last Man Standing, I'm sure that the similarities are entirely coincidental. In true red top style, the stories invariably mocked Alex; highlighting problems with his health and training regime.

Alex Reid: The Fight of his Life hit the TV screens on April 12th. Episode one saw our hero travel to Valencia to see if the offbeat Keysi fighting system would be useful in his fight. I think you can guess the answer. In the next couple, Alex went to India, so he could be photographed in a loin cloth, and San Diego, where he met some capoeira dude who was on a weird black power tip. So far, nothing for Tom to lose sleep over.

In the fourth chapter, Alex rolled up at Combat Submission Wrestling in Fullerton, California. Now, he had my attention. CSW is the home of Erik Paulson, the man who is responsible for teaching the modern MMA world about the potency of catch wrestling. A few minutes into the show, Josh Barnett walked in and told Alex he was going to tutor him in 'old Wigan style' wrestling. This was going to be ace. Access to a training session at one of the world's top gyms. Masters of the lost art showing the old country the tricks of their ancestors. It may even help Alex in his fight.

The excitement lasted a few minutes then Alex went on a pointless trip to work out with the US Marine Corps. The kind of thing you do if you're more concerned with making a dumb TV show than preparing for a fight. Alex aggravated a knee injury and the fight was in doubt.

This wasn't a shock to MMA fans. Three days after the first episode aired, Tom Watson started a thread on the cagewarriors.com forum entitled:

'Alex Reid Pulls Out From The Fight'.

- I have just found out this news and have posted the information on my blog.

Just to make this clear I WILL NEVER SIGN TO FIGHT ALEX AGAIN after the way he has behaved with such lack of respect. No amount of money can make me waste my time in preparing to fight him again.

I wanted to release this on cagewarriors first so the MMA community was the first to know and could get the real truth before the media goes crazy.

Hopefully another much tougher opponent will be announced soon.

Tom

The reaction was a tidal wave of 'I told you so' posts. Outside of his close friends and family, it is fair to say most people were sceptical about the Alex's convenient injury.

From the lowest level, UK MMA is bedevilled by bullshit pullouts. Whether it's guys getting a better offer or simple bottle jobs, cards regularly fall apart as a result of them. All that week, Alex Reid and Jordan were pictured in the papers sunning themselves on a luxury vacation in Egypt. For the hanging jury, this was proof positive. Alex Reid had gone soft. He'd sold out.

Those who had opposed the fight all along were now inexplicably furious that it wasn't happening. As Alex was now a celeb, the red tops all stuck the boot in. Alex Reid was done as far as the UK MMA scene was concerned.

Persona non grata in one of the world's least reputable and non-exclusive clubs.

BAMMA had concentrated all their marketing on the Alex Reid angle. Banking on a huge interest from the Jordan massive, they had booked the cavernous LG Arena- a way bigger space than any domestic promotion required. To everyone's amazement, the event was going ahead. Matt Horwich was named as Reid's replacement in the main event. For Tom Watson, this was a better fight. Horwich had a name in the States thanks to his exploits in the now defunct International Fight League and was known as a tough wrestler. If 'Kong' could deal with him, it would underline his progression and make him a more attractive proposition for the big shows.

Fight day at the Crowne Plaza Hotel, NEC branch. In the corner of the bar Tom Watson was looking relaxed with a bunch of his mates. Amid the usual faces you see on the fringes of any UK show was a crew of patched up German Hells Angels. On the far side, the FA Cup final was on TV. The last hurrah for Pompey. There were groans when Kevin Prince Boateng missed a penalty. There was to be no fairy tale ending. Portsmouth had been living beyond their means for years. Now economic reality had caught up with them. Administration and relegation followed and survival as a football club was far from guaranteed. From all the talk, they were not the only sporting organisation on the verge of folding.

BLOODY REVOLUTION

On the walk to the venue, I didn't see a soul. Outside the arena, the leading lights of the MMA press pack were enjoying the sunshine. Normally the topic of conversation would be the fights, with everyone vying to prove how in the know they were. That day, it was all about the money.

The forums were full of stories about BAMMA dishing out stacks of free tickets. The tales were put about by folks with connections to rival promotions, but that didn't mean they weren't true. Papering the house to fill embarrassing gaps is standard practice. The trick is to do it on the sly so that paying customers don't get the hump. On paper, the card was strong: three title bouts plus a couple of popular American imports. Without the main event BAMMA had spent the last six months hyping, would anyone be there to see it?

Inside the LG Arena, the atmosphere was eerie. The undercard fights played out in near silence. Huge banks of empty seats disappeared back into the darkness. No expense had been spared on the production, but it didn't seem quite right. The background of the promoters was evident. The runners were keen young lasses decked out in black. All night they buzzed about, keeping the many suits supplied with bottled water and slices of pizza. This was the kind of scene that would look more at home on a film set than at a fight night.

A downmarket colleague on press row told me that one of the ring girls was Rhian Sugden. When he clocked my blank look, he explained that she was the girl who had been in the papers for exchanging saucy texts with Vernon Kay. Making the position of ring girl even cheaper- only media bods could manage that.

The Frankfurt chapter of the Hells Angels strolled in and occupied a row of cageside seats. I don't know if they'd paid for them, but no one was going to ask them to leave. On the other side of the cage, Tom Watson's fans were livening up. Wherever Kong fights he brings a huge, rowdy following, many of them packing outsized inflat- able bananas. After the tempestuous build up, I was expecting something extra.

A couple of weeks earlier, his mate John had turned up to the long awaited premiere of Killer Bitch in a T-shirt bearing the legend: 'Team Kong, Alex Reid bottled it'. This was a mere starter for his gloriously extreme effort at BAMMA 3.

John appeared dressed as Jordan; with a long flowing drag queen wig, shades and a figure hugging little black dress. He was pushing a wheelchair containing a man in a gorilla suit. So that nobody would miss the injury refer- ence, the ape was wearing a shirt that said: 'I am Alex Reid'. The Frankfurt Angels looked mystified as fake Jordan simulated a sex act with a banana in front of a gaggle of amateur photographers. There were a couple of women knocking about with microphones. Someone told me they were making a 'cage fighting' documentary for BBC Radio 4. If they use this occurrence as an example of normal crowd behaviour, their programme will be a strange piece of work.

The fights themselves were great. In Jude Samuel, BAMMA had a matchmaker who understood the game and had put together a set of well balanced contests. He must have popped out for a coffee when the original main event was suggested.

For all the positives, the story was the lack of a crowd. It's hard to be sure but, even allowing for freebies, I'd guess that there were considerably less than a thousand in. It seemed like most of them came down stairs to get a photo of the only genuine superstar to make an appearance. Georges St. Pierre was a training partner of Tom Watson and he'd come over to support his man. His interval interview with Christian O'Connell created more excitement in the hall than the fights that preceded it. Another sign of the dominant position enjoyed by the UFC.

The crowd returned to their slumber when the action recommenced. During the Featherweight title bout between Alan Omer and Mark Adams, it was silent apart from the Adams' fans applauding their man's control on the ground. In an instant, the mood changed. Alex Reid and Jordan turned up. With full entourage in tow, they swept into a row of cageside seats. Tumult replaced indifference. The crowd stood as one. Camera flashes exploded out of the darkness with total disregard for the fighters in the cage.

The fights became a sideshow next to the full blown pantomime in the crowd. Cageside, the jeering seemed good humoured. A couple of inflatable bananas headed towards the happy couple as well as a few choice gestures. Security took steps to prevent anyone getting too close to them. The chanting came from the back of the hall.

Being in a crowd, even one as sparse as the BAMMA 3 mob, gives individuals the chance to spout their worst freely. It was hard to make out the faces in the darkness, but I'd guess they were normal, celeb obsessed British citizens. The songs varied slightly, but the delivery was the same. Laughing fake jollity masking a more sinister, hateful sentiment.

-ALEX IS A PUSSY:

understandable in the circumstances.

-JORDAN WEARS A STRAP ON:

a more personal extension of the former.

-JORDAN WANTS A GANG BANG:

the voice of fuckwits united.

For all their protestations, the suckers couldn't get enough of her. Jordan and her posse went to go to the bar. All eyes left the fight and followed her. All except the Frankfurt Hells Angels. They were all about the violence and seemed slightly bemused by the attention this odd looking lady was attracting.

Matt Horwich came out for the main event. Outwardly, he had the demeanour of a trendy vicar as he calmly strolled in brandishing the bible, but peace and love were not on his agenda. By any measure, he was a superior fighter to Alex Reid, with impressive wrestling and a zany, Eddie Bravo inspired submission game. This had all the makings of an intriguing contest. It was one of the best match ups of the year on British soil but the atmosphere was flat. Most of the crowd were more preoccupied with the whereabouts of a former topless model.

Watson's entrance gave them a lift. He'd been in the Daily Star and everything so he was nearly a celebrity too. He wore an outsized sombrero over his regular gorilla mask and danced in time to a Latin accompaniment. Georges St. Pierre followed him in carrying a hybrid England and Quebec flag. After the insanity generated by some of the punters, it all seemed rather low key.

The fight was twenty five minutes of grit and grind. Horwich's game plan was: get it to the fence and take him down. He followed it to perfection in the first then applied a convincing rear naked choke. On the big screen, Watson's eyes had the serene look of a man on the way out, but he dug deep and broke free. In the second, Tom had more success, landing some meaty body shots. The third was a clinch war against the fence. When the pair separated, Watson tagged Horwich with a big right hand and the American looked in trouble for the first time. Horwich fired back in the fourth. His takedowns and ground control forced Kong to give his back as he struggled to get up. Tight against the cage, Horwich launched another convincing rear naked choke attempt. In the final round, the boys were back on the canvas with Matt in charge. Tom managed to reverse the position and unleashed some solid ground and pound.

Most of the press pack had Matt Horwich down as the winner, some of them giving it to him by a couple of rounds. I had Tom Watson edging it by a round.

When judging a fight, I always exercise a little doublethink; tot up the correct result and the likely result. The best outcome for BAMMA was a Watson win. Horwich had a style that would never sell a ticket in the UK. Tom was marketable and had benefited from the hype when Alex was still in the picture. I'm not saying the judges are bent. They are human. People like to be nice to people who have been nice to them. There's no governing body to answer to, you get appointed by the promoters. They pay your wage and they pay for your nice hotel. Why cause them a headache?

The judges scored the fight unanimously for Watson. One agreed with my assessment of the likely result, 48-47. Another made it 49-47. The third judge must have really enjoyed his buffet breakfast and saw it 49-46 through his union jack specs. Tom Watson was the BAMMA Middleweight champion. Would he ever get to defend his belt?

BAMMA got killed on the gate. All their eggs had been in the basket that Alex Reid dropped on a US Marine base. According to the Wikipedia page for the BAMMA 3 event, the attendance was 5,000. Follow the reference link and, instead of getting a report, you get the results and a reminder to watch the event on TV. Facts are a rare commodity these days. Sometimes, you think you've tracked one of the critters down, then you find out it's a lump of cunningly disguised marketing bullshit.

Lots of MMA insiders had been down on BAMMA for a while. No doubt, some of the bad words were coming from rivals. The leading lights of Ultimate Challenge had left in acrimonious circumstances after the first BAMMA show and plenty of those who had been involved in the BFC blamed the upstart promotion for its demise. In all the black propaganda, gossip and hearsay, there was a recurring refrain; they don't know what they're doing. They had come into a sport they did not understand to cash in, ignored the advice of experts and were sure to come a cropper.

Along with Horwich, two other Americans had been flown over. Seth Petruzelli, the man who knocked out Kimbo Slice to sink EliteXC, and War Machine.

War had been born Jon Koppenhaver but legally changed his name to War Machine. He had made his name on The Ultimate Fighter and then remained in the headlines due to his colourful lifestyle. War was dropped by major promotions after making off message comments on social networking sites. The UFC didn't like his comments about the death of former champion Evan Tanner and a blog entry that slagged off Barack Obama got him the bullet from Bellator. War continued to fight successfully on the small show circuit, but became better known for his out of cage activities: specifically being a porn star and getting arrested for violent felonies. In November 2009, he managed to combine both of these hobbies. After attending a porn actress's birthday party, he made this now legendary posting on Twitter:

- Fuck...last night was NOT good...lil' misunderstanding and then WM was back in effect and the bodies hit the floor. I'm fucked...Pretty sure my porn days are over. Prolly be going to jail too...when they find me...haha.

War would land in jail eventually, but not for that escapade and not before he had the chance to fight on BAMMA 3.

In Birmingham, he was a shadow of his former, hell-raising self. Quiet and polite, you wouldn't have recognized him if it hadn't been for the hand grenade tattooed on his hand. Seth and War both claimed easy first round victories. War fell victim to the ash cloud revival and had to hang around in Brum for a few days. The highlight of his stay was his Twitter appeal for fans to phone in fake orders to a pizza place that he felt had done him wrong. It seemed so quaint coming from the man who once had a bag put over his head by San Diego police officers to stop him from spitting on them whilst they arrested him on suspicion of assault with a deadly weapon.

All good fun, but War Machine's fondness for sharing his views with the world would soon backfire on BAMMA.

BLOODY REVOLUTION

He started tweeting about not getting paid. Seth Petruzelli also started to pop up on the net asking when he was going to get his dough. Even Matt Horwich, the man who had stepped up at short notice to give the show a main event, was going short. His wife turned up on the Underground forum three weeks after the fight demanding to know where the money was. The silence from BAMMA was deafening.

Eventually, the fighters were paid, but the damage was done. The general consensus was that BAMMA were done for. Them and their big ideas. They'd spunked six figures on a show and had come nowhere near the breakthrough they were hoping for. There was a lot of barely concealed gloating from the old timers. These newbies had come into their game and tried to tell them how it's done. Thanks for stopping by. Don't let the door hit your arse on the way out.

ACT II

Six weeks after the shenanigans at the LG Arena, BAMMA called a press conference at a club in Covent Garden. The spiel was polished and brazen. BAMMA 3 had been a massive success. Now they were stepping it up a notch with BAMMA 4. At the 12,000 seater National Indoor Arena, in the heart of Birmingham, and live on Bravo TV- Alex Reid would take on Tom Watson in 'the fight we've all been waiting for'.

Yup, they were going again. One by one, the three men at the top table said their pieces. In the centre, wearing a white shirt and black tie, was David Green of Giant TV. After kicking off, he handed over to matchmaker Jude Samuel. Jude talked about the quality of the match ups at the last show and his hopes for the next instalment. You couldn't argue with what he was saying. He had put together a brilliant set of fights and the choice of imports was inspired, undoubtedly an artistic triumph, but what about the empty seats and the lack of wages? If he'd been pitching this on Dragon's Den- this would be the point where Duncan Bannatyne tells him he's a lovely guy, what he's doing is great- but it is not a business, it's not going to make any money and this is why he's out.

Next up was Alex Reid. He spoke of his desire to prove his worth. That he was not a celebrity, he was a fighter. Alex stumbled through a series of clichés as he talked about his hunger to succeed and his new found intensity in the gym. He knew that he had lost a lot of credibility in the fight game and he was determined to show he was more than the bloke who stands next to Jordan in pictures.

As Kojak told us, a picture paints a thousand words. Being in the pictures biz, Giant TV know this better than most; David Green was Clothes Show Model of the Year 1990 for crying out loud. They must have been aware of the message the presser layout was sending. The last show had been wrecked by the no show of one of the principals. Tom Watson had publicly stated that Reid was a joke and he would not fight him again for any amount of money. This time round, Alex was in the house but Tom wasn't. Not in the flesh anyway.

Tom was in Albuquerque. He joined via video link, showing the level of respect he had for the affair by crouching over a laptop with no shirt on. When questioned about the fight he was candid.

- I won't prepare for Alex specifically as an opponent because I did that last time and we saw what happened there.

In a couple of weeks, Tom was due back in the country for a Thai fight, but he did not make the effort to come early for the press conference. Bare-chested and sweaty, he spelled it out for the gathered journos. He was expected to win because he was a dedicated athlete who took his work seriously. He had put together a good run of results, unlike Alex who had not had an MMA fight for three years and had not won one for five. Basically, Alex had not earned the right to fight him.

This was not good for BAMMA. Trash talk sells tickets. A calm analysis of why the main event is a hopeless mismatch is less helpful. When the champion can't be arsed to turn up to help hype the supposed mega fight, the alarm bells start ringing.

Alex had been stung by the criticism and disrespect he'd been getting from the MMA community; the place he used to call home. Behind his laboured soundbites about wanting to inspire the audience, he seemed genuinely up for the fight. Tom's manner screamed contractual obligation.

Alex bit. He was sick of not being taken seriously. He was Alex fucking Reid: MMA pioneer. He fired back.

- Are you fighting me for a bit of celebrity? Or are you fighting me to shut me up? Or are you fighting me for MMA? I don't get it.

Tom responded.

- I fight because I have the belt and BAMMA want me to fight you. Don't get too arrogant brother- I'll fight whoever they want. If they change you tomorrow, I ain't gonna lose any sleep about it.

Ten days after the press conference, Tom announced his next fight. He was going to take on Danillo Villefort at MFC 26 in Brandon, Manitoba. Villefort had UFC and WEC experience and an impressive paper record, but he was undersized at Middleweight and could be stopped. This made sense in every way the Reid fight didn't. In terms of career progression, a win over Villefort would demonstrate that Tom was definitely ready for the major international shows. A loss would not be the end of the world as the Brazilian BJJ black belt was legit.

All well and good, but one thing cried out for attention. The date of the fight: 10th September 2010- fifteen days before BAMMA 4. Fifteen days before the fight that was being billed as the biggest in UK history. Hardly ideal preparation, taking a tougher fight on another continent two weeks out. Add in the potential to pick up an injury and this looked like a convenient way out of the fight. A chance to make real strides careerwise and leave the Alex Reid nonsense behind. Tom had already got his name out there in the publicity leading up to the first scheduled fight. It was debatable how much extra recognition he could squeeze out of actually fighting Alex.

Two weeks later, MFC switched Tom's opponent. He was now due to fight Jesse Taylor. The stakes were raised. Jesse Taylor was something that Alex Reid could only dream of being: a reality TV star that people had heard of in North America. Taylor came to prominence in the seventh season of The Ultimate Fighter. The junk food guzzling wrestler advanced to the final after a series of forceful but dull wins. Success went to his head. On a drunken night out in Vegas, Jesse was caught on CCTV kicking in a limo window. It was also alleged that he continued to be out of order inside a hotel; intimidating the staff and giving it large about being a UFC fighter. Word got back to Zuffa and Taylor was kicked out of the finale.

This was a tragedy for Jesse and a result for the UFC. Taylor was an accomplished wrestler. He had the ability to take men down and control them on the canvas, but showed neither the inclination nor the capability to finish them off. Jesse was a master of lay and pray- the combat sports equivalent of mogadon. Firing him allowed the UFC to take the moral high ground and meant they did not have to feature a man who was box office poison. This had all happened in 2008. In the two years since, Taylor had stayed active. He was no joke and win over him would get Tom noticed by the people who matter.

BLOODY REVOLUTION

While this political drama was rumbling along, lighter rations were being served up by ITV 2. Katie and Alex: For Better For Worse was a three part look at the marriage of the Elizabeth Taylor and Richard Burton of the Live From Studio Five epoch. The show followed the couple as they had their wedding blessed in their local village church. Throughout the piece, there was a running theme- the couple's struggle to keep their lives private. Yes, you read that right. Two people who are famous only for having their photographs in the popular press spent three hours moaning about how they just wanted to be alone. The fact that this was played straight is testament to the power of Jordan.

Her reality shows follow the glorious leader's line whatever the evidence to the contrary. For instance, in another show, Jordan released a single that bombed miserably and played a gig where a large section of the audience was openly hostile. The voice over harped on about how this disaster was actually a triumph. In contrast, Alex is usually portrayed as an amiable tool on TV: a hapless individual who plays house while his memsahib deals with the matters of importance.

Alex is a major supporting character in the Jordan shows, but the favour is never returned. We never see a hair of her head in his Bravo efforts. Even in situations where she is certainly present, great care is taken to edit her out. Jordan/Katie is too big of a deal to give her image away for free.

Katie and Alex: For Better For Worse produced some moments which were way beyond parody. Before the wedding blessing, friends of the couple gave sincere speeches about how this was a private day which was being ruined by the paparazzi pack who wanted to take pictures. As they were telling all this to a film crew who were recording the private day so it could be broadcast to the nation, you kept waiting for them to start giggling and admitting they were taking the piss. But they didn't.

The doublethink got even tougher on honeymoon. Alex and Katie had gone to a remote Thai hideaway to get away from it all. Just the two lovebirds and their ITV 2 camera crew. In the finished programme, they are constantly wary of being caught on camera, except of course the TV camera they had an exclusive deal with. This mind boggling slice of faux reality reportedly netted them £600,000.

BAMMA 4 minus 21 days.
Tom 'Kong' Watson v Jesse 'JT Money' Taylor minus six days.

I was in Bolton following the career of another reality TV star. Dane Bowers finished second to Alex in Celebrity Big Brother 9. As he was an ex-boyfriend of Jordan, the producers no doubt expected him to clash with Alex, but instead, they did what nice guys do and just got along.

On the outside, Dane was involved with KnuckleUp. After a few well received efforts in the South West, they decided they were ready to take the show on the road. Them, BAMMA and a few others had decided it was time to take UK MMA to Another Level. They figured that there was sufficient interest to sell shows on the basis of talent alone. Leave behind the notion of regional shows that rely on local ticket sellers to put on productions that would appeal to MMA fans. The build it and they will come approach. 'You're out of your mind' protested hard boiled veterans of the scene, but they were wasting their time.

KnuckleUp headed to London and found the streets were not paved with gold. Their show scheduled for Billingsgate in June had been pulled at the last minute because of poor ticket sales. They were not alone.

In April, hoping to carry on where their Norwich debut had left off, Bushido Challenge had gone to Nottingham to put on a card featuring some of the best fighters on the circuit. Both shows were smash hits with the press, fighters and trainers. Unfortunately, only two men and a dog paid to see them and BC 3 was on hold indefinitely.

Ignoring the setbacks, KnuckleUp soldiered on with their grand plan. Their next show was Kings of the North at the Bolton Arena. Bolton was the home turf of Fight Ikon. Greater Manchester was also home to the growing Ultimate Cage Challenge and just the week before Ireland's Cage Contender had put on a card in Altrincham (the latter event is now best known as the night Ricky Hatton got filmed snorting coke at the hotel afterwards). A short hop away in Liverpool was Chris Zorba's OMMAC.

In short, bringing a new show to the North West was ambitious bordering on insanity. But MMA is going to be the next big thing- right?

The Bolton show was a disappointment on every level. For a variety of reasons, the card fell apart. Of the eight contests that survived, only one went past the first round, meaning the few people who had turned up were rewarded with regular, elongated breaks. These were filled with head shaking and small talk about the folly of the enterprise. Even during the fights, the atmosphere barely surpassed tumbleweed level. Dane was in the cage, doing the post fight interviews. He's good at it, but the cracks were showing. It's hard to be a cheeky chappy on the mic when your show is collapsing around you.

Things got worse. In the weeks after the event, fighters started popping up on forums asking where their money was. The same cash flow problems that had hit BAMMA were obviously catching.

Soon after, the much talked about Kudegra promotion tanked. Launched with big ideas, they had pretensions of starting at the top. Kudegra were going to put on a show every month with tournament formats leading to the crowning of national champions. Everything was in place; huge venues like Sheffield Arena, a host of respected names and bumper guaranteed wage packets for fighters who went all the way. Even by the standards of the UK MMA scene, Kudegra set new standards in terms of talking the talk then failing to walk the walk. Key personnel jumped ship, the money dried up and all of their impressive (on paper) programmed events were suspended.

The holy grail of a sustainable national show appeared to be an impossible dream. With a network of established local shows that fed star performers straight to the UFC leviathan, was there really a gap in the market? One by one, the pretenders fell. Of the latest crop, only BAMMA was still standing.

The Watson / Taylor fight was a headache for BAMMA. In interviews, Tom had stressed that this was his priority. He was focusing on the job in hand and had put all thoughts of Alex Reid to one side. Any kind of injury would surely rule him out of the Reid fight. After ten months of hype, did BAMMA have a plan B or would this be the last straw? As is so often the case, the behind the scenes intrigue was more compelling than the fight itself.

The internet is nothing short of miraculous. Two decades ago, we had four TV channels that shut down around midnight. Now, it is possible to get live coverage of just about any sporting event on the planet with a few mouse clicks.

With freedom comes responsibility. If you are in the business of reporting on the sport, you have to be hip to every development as it happens. So here I was again, in my role as a messenger at the vanguard of the information revolution- surrounded by empty bottles of Becks, cursing at a laptop in the early hours of the morning.

Finding a serviceable stream was not proving as easy as usual. The Shine Fights Lightweight tournament was going on in Oklahoma and most of my regular haunts had opted to put that up instead of the MFC card. I hit on a stream from Canada but abandoned it; too jerky; more a collection of stills than a video representation. Fight time was looming and I had nothing. I was frantically scanning streaming sites when I hit pay dirt. A clear image of a man in a gorilla mask dancing to the Sir Mix-A-Lot classic Jump On It. Let's get it on.

The first round is predictable: JT shooting for take-downs, Watson trying to keep on his feet at all costs. This any means necessary strategy leads to the ref instructing the judges to dock a point for persistently holding onto the ropes of the MFC ring. Jesse shoots again, the sound on my stream starts fading, the picture freezes then blacks out.

After five minutes of frantic searching, I reconnect with Manitoba. The second round is coming to a close. They show a replay of Tom resisting a rear naked choke and the consensus in the booth is another round for Taylor. Kong needs a stoppage to win. The third is the same old story. Jesse looks tired. He is content to take his man down and use his superior wrestling to run down the clock. Tom has chances to get up, but does not take them. The commentator cannot hide his frustration.

- I want to slap him with a wet fish.

The final bell sounds. The scores are 30-26 across the board. Another example of the UK's wrestling deficit. Tom has been over in North America for years addressing this, but catching up ain't that simple. People like Taylor have been doing this their whole lives. The winner is on the mic.

- Let's party tonight Canada.

His rallying call is met by silence. Wrestlers are effective but hard to love. The result is not really what I was interested in. Tom took little in the way of punishment. Although you can never be certain, it looked as though he had come through the fight unscathed. With a bit of luck- he would be good to go for BAMMA 4.

Some of the main players had different fortunes in TV land. Five days after the Kong/JT fight, Bravo got knocked out. BskyB announced that it was reviewing its offerings to the masses. The laddish Bravo was getting the axe. BAMMA 4 was safe, but the long term prospects were uncertain.

If you talked to any UK promoter for long enough, they would give you a sob story about TV. Often it would involve some dark mutterings about BAMMA. The word around the camp fire was they had taken terms that were so ridiculously uncompetitive to get their show on TV, it was costing them money. No doubt, the plan was to benefit long term by establishing themselves as the highest profile UK show. Now the devil they had done the deal with was getting the chop, the future was uncertain.

It may be a blow for MMA, but Alex Reid wouldn't be going short. BskyB had decided to channel their resources into Living TV instead. Living's biggest signing: Katie Price.

In June, they had done an exclusive two year deal with her production company reportedly worth £10 million. ITV were dischuffed about their prize asset defecting so they had not been promoting the new series of her reality show. Price was doing the rounds to do her own publicity.

In the week before the fight, she popped up on the puerile panel programme Celebrity Juice. During the show, there were a few references to Alex's cross dressing- the thing he is most famous for in tabloid land. Towards the end, Katie showed the star quality that Living were paying the big bucks for.

Comedy misogynist Keith Lemon asked the team captains, Fearne Cotton and Holly Willoughby, if they would consider lezzing it up with Kim Kardashian. Most of the show is based on the host making smutty suggestions to the team captains and them reacting like the posh, jolly hockey sticks types they are. Lemon then asked Katie the same question. Her response:

- I'd lick her out all day long.

That is what gets you a multi million pound contract in UK 2010. Forget talent: if you're willing to slag it up for the boys in the cheap seats you've got it made.

BLOODY REVOLUTION

Tom Watson was operating on a different level. Two days before the fight he sent a profound question out to the world via his Twitter account:

- Anyone else think it's crazy that man hasn't set foot on the moon since 1972.

ACT THREE

Birmingham- city on the move. The second city was putting on a massive event to show what they were all about. An event that would present the place in a new light and let the world know that this is a destination fit for the 21st century. In late September 2010, posters featuring the grinning visage of a minor celebrity who had been hand picked to be the face of the show adorned every spare inch of the city centre. I saw him in person on the Friday afternoon.

George Lamb was the host and poster boy of Style Birmingham Live: three days of catwalk fashion shows and beauty events organised by Retail Birmingham. Motown UK wanted to throw off the oil and grease of the old days and cover itself in lippy and designer threads. Better go heavy on the foundation to hide the cracks.

Lamb was being interviewed next to the Harvey Nichol's hub- a temporary structure in Victoria Square. He was carefully positioned to make sure that he was next to the Harvey Nichols logo in any shot. Was this a news crew or was it marketing? What's the difference these days?

A crowd started to gather: most were just staring but plenty were pulling out their mobiles to snap a picture. A couple of the amateur photographers peeled away as I was passing. One asked the other who they'd just papped. She said she thought he was an actor. I think she'd got him mixed up with somebody else, but I wasn't certain. I knew he'd been on the radio, although I'd never heard his show, and I knew his dad was a baddie in Eastenders and a goodie in Gavin and Stacey. He may be an actor. Who cares? He's a celebrity; a white guy who looks good in a suit- the perfect ambassador for Brum's transition from city of substance to city of style.

I was en route to the other celebrity happening of the day; the BAMMA 4 weigh in. To get to the National Indoor Arena, I had to walk through the heart of New Birmingham; past the ICC, which would host the Tory Party conference the following week. Perhaps the most glaring example of style over substance. All David Cameron has ever done since leaving school is spin and polish for political gain. Not that the other parties are any different of course. Rule by a bunch of talentless, celebrity white guys who look good in suits: Media-ocracy. Mediocrity.

I arrived at the Olympian Suite with time to spare. The joint was set up for business. Rows of chairs for the press facing the scales and some grander chairs behind a BAMMA bannered table. And, of course, there were some scales. Usually, this kind of gig is managed by rough guys in T-shirts and trackie bottoms. The BAMMA crew were more lounge suit kind of guys with accents that hinted at second division public schools.

The fighters were being ushered into an adjoining room, ready to be called for their turn on the scales. Tom Watson was out front, wrapped up in his training gear while he shadow boxed. He was going to be OK. If he had any worries about his weight, he'd be sweating it off away from prying eyes.

I started circulating to get the gossip. John Philips, the Welsh slugger who was looking for a title shot, was rumoured to be way over. This was unfortunate. He was being talked up as the next big thing thanks to his all action style, but he was also getting a reputation for missing the weight. With ten minutes to the official weigh in time, there were two no shows: Philips' opponent, James Zikic, and Alex Reid.

Without the star attraction, the weigh in went ahead on time. In the time honoured and tiresome tradition, the pairs of fighters stripped down to novelty underpants before getting on the scales then squaring up for a photo.

The first man to have an issue was Scott Jansen. The muscular Cockney had cheekbones like Ronnie Wood's when he stood on the scales. He looked down with an air of resignation. 156 ½. The Lightweight limit is 155, but you're allowed a pound over. Scott was informed he had one hour to lose the offending half a pound. He shuffled off with his head down; a healthy young athlete moving with the vim and vigour of a sedated pensioner. That's what weight cutting will do to you.

Jansen was following a trend. For decades, hard bitten boxers have been boiling down to the bare minimum their body can stand in order to give themselves a competitive advantage. As the years go by, they are forced up the divisions as they develop physically. In MMA, the traffic has flowed in the other direction.

The message sent out by the early UFCs was that weight was not as much of an issue in the cage. Over the years, the influx of money into the sport encouraged fighters to do anything to gain an edge. In short, they became professionals. Jansen had previously operated at Welterweight but had dropped a division. Talk to any fighter and making weight is the thing they hate the most. Throughout a training camp: dieting, eating clean, drinking gallons of liquids and taking an array of supplements are as important as hitting pads. The final week is the killer. Over the last few days, starvation rations are in effect and the plentiful liquid supply is cut off. Every ounce of water weight is burnt off, often fully clothed in an onsite sauna, to leave a bag of bones and muscle at the weigh in.

Ideally, a fighter will only hit the magic number at the time of the weigh in. Once he gets off the scales, the zombie is led away to be re-energised. It is common for a fighter to weigh a stone over his declared weight when he finally enters the cage. For most lads, the preferred method of achieving this nutritional miracle is a taxi to the nearest Nandos. It's a reward to put them in a good state of mind. A sign that the hard work is in the bank and it's time to get pumped up before battle commences. Scott would have to wait a little longer for his trip to chicken heaven.

The rest were weighing in with no visible problems. We were on to the featured bouts. Eugene Fadiora against Gunnar Nelson was the fight with the most at stake. Fadiora was an unbeaten prospect who was making people sit up and take notice in the UK. Icelander Gunnar Nelson was making people stand up and say wow across the MMA blogoshphere. The 22 year old's exploits in jiu jitsu tournaments were already the stuff of legend, particularly his victory over the monster that is Jeff Monson.

Eugene hit his number on the button, like good pro's do. Gunnar was up next. It was hard to believe this quiet youngster was the same guy who was ready to terrorise the Welterweight division. He seemed to sleepwalk through everything he did. On the scales, Nelson stared impassively. His face was expressionless. It reminded me of the mugshots you see on TV when a Scandinavian black metal band have been captured after going over the edge and embarking on a rampage of church arson and ritual nun slaying. He knew the terrible suffering he was capable of inflicting and he was cool with it.

The pair posed: shirts off, fists up. Someone asked Gunnar for a prediction. He replied in the lyrical fashion that only speakers of a foreign language can achieve:

- This will be a dandy.

With that, Gunnar put his hoodie back on then nonchalantly wandered off with his crew.

Previews of BAMMA 4 by MMA pundits based outside the UK had spent about ten seconds on the main event then devoted their attention to Nelson v Fadiora. Gunnar was undoubtedly the draw, but a quick scan of Eugene's record would tell anyone he was no joke. There was a theme running through all the analysis: the winner will be in line for a UFC contract. Herein lurks the dilemma for any UK promotion with aspirations of going mainstream.

The way the sport has developed means that the UFC is so far above everyone else in terms of prestige and exposure, it is the expected destination for any fighter on the up. It's just the way it is. Any discussion of a prospect's merits is based on how far away he is from getting a UFC contract. Once there, a fighter is judged on his proximity to the title or, horror of horrors, getting cut and sent back down to a small pond.

A show like BAMMA can have all the trappings of a big show, it originally billed itself as the 'Fighting Premiership', but the reality is something else. As things stand, it can only be a feeder show: sort of the fighting Championship or, probably more accurately, the fighting League One.

James Zikic was still not in the house. John Philips stripped and got on the scales. He looked down at the number more in hope than expectation. 189 lbs. He had one hour to lose 3lbs. There was no panic. His team knew he was going to miss. They went off to do the best they could.

It was Reidernator time, but the Reidernator wasn't there. Tom Watson weighed in a pound under then got dressed with no fuss. Without Alex Reid, the idea of a proper press conference became redundant. What a waste of fancy chairs and a banner.

The MC gave a quick spiel on the mic then opened up to questions from the floor. He was greeted by silence. From the back, BAMMA's media guy piped up to create the illusion of press interest in the fight.

- How do you feel about Alex not being present?

Tom shrugged. He made a little crack about him maybe being too much of a superstar to weigh in at the proper time then went on to say he didn't want to say too much in case there was a genuine excuse for the no show. With that, the Q & A was wound up. Tom sat down in a corner and got into a packet of crisps and a can of coconut drink. He left a few minutes later. The rest of us waited.

Over the sixty minutes, Scott Jansen came back and made weight... and that's about it. Everyone else pretended to be doing something: writing up notes, deleting texts, tidying tables. Anything to pretend you weren't being made a mug of. With the hour nearly over, John Philips returned. He was still the best part of a pound over. At 4 o'clock, an announcement was made. Alex Reid, James Zikic and John Philips had officially missed weight.

James Zikic arrived at seven minutes past the hour. He had taken a train up from London and got a taxi from New Street to the arena in plenty of time. Unfortunately, the cab driver had taken him to the arena at the NEC and he'd had to get another one back through the worst of the Brum traffic.

He jumped on the scales and weighed in at 184 lbs. He was informed that Philips had not made the weight. Did he still want to fight? He looked non-plussed. Zikic was an old stager; have gloves will travel. Not fighting never occurred to him.

He and John faced off for the photos. As soon as they broke their pose, John shook his hand and thanked him. James nodded. That was everyone weighed in. All except the one man who the entire show had been built around.

It is impossible to revisit boredom. You look back on it, and it doesn't seem so bad. After all, it was only a sitting around on a chair for a few hours. And there was the music.

To add a little verve, someone had compiled a mixtape to accompany the weigh in: Welcome to the Jungle, Harder- Faster- Stronger, Paranoid, Fix Up- Look Sharp and Sabotage. A lot of thought had gone into it: belligerent rock anthem, commercial hip hop, local heroes, contemporary classic and a mix of all the above. What started as a pleasant distraction turned into a symbol of our torment. Every time Slash cranked out the intro, we knew we'd completed another cycle of nothing. It was soul destroying stuff. As Dr Samuel Johnson once noted: 'when a man is tired of Black Sabbath, he is tired of life.'

I got chatting to one of the cameramen. He told me he'd been at the BAMMA event at the Bullring the week before. It was billed as a face off between Tom and Alex followed by a competition to select a ring girl. The snapper was enthusiastic. He said there were loads of people there...it was absolutely packed...most of them didn't know what was going on. Like most great ideas in UK MMA, the more you probed it, the less impressive it was. Firm breasts, skimpy knickers and a celeb may pull you a crowd and get you some press but they don't help you to convince the world you are a serious proposition. Like the George Lamb watchers, most of the drones had probably wandered away none the wiser.

BLOODY REVOLUTION

Every now and then, an unconfirmed snippet of info sweeps through the room.

- Alex is three miles away.

- He'll be here any time.

- Alex is 10 minutes away.

There was no plan B. The idea that BAMMA would even consider pulling the fight was ridiculous. If Alex Reid turned up weighing 40 stone, the fight would go ahead. If he didn't bother turning up at all- ditto. He had them over a barrel; he knew it and they knew it. Everyone with a BAMMA connection was doing their best to hide their irritation but it was oozing out of them.

It was about quarter to six, knocking on for three hours after the official weigh in started. I was over by the window, reading the empty drinks can that Tom Watson left behind. It really had come to that. Out of the corner of my eye, I saw a small group crossing the canal bridge. One of them was the unmistakeable figure of Jeremy 'Bad Boy' Bailey' resplendent in a sky blue tracksuit. He was with three others, one of them wrapped in bulky sweats with the hood up. It had to be him. I alerted the room.

- He's here

Marc Goddard was the head of rules. For the duration of the wait, he had maintained an air of calm professionalism as traces of steam shot out of his ears. He came over and looked through the blinds at the very moment the party disappeared behind a bush. There had been a few bogus sightings and he gave me a look that would melt ice. I assured him I was on the level and they reappeared a second later.

Alex Reid walked into the Olympian Suite and headed straight for the bogs with his entourage. This looked bad. He must be trying to squeeze out the last drop of liquid before getting on the scales. Alex emerged a few minutes later; naked with a towel round him; another sign that he was not confident of making weight. He tossed off an apology to no one in particular about bad traffic.

Everyone was pissed off about the contempt he'd treated the occasion with but also relieved that he'd actually bothered to come in the end. Bailey and Goddard held up the towel to hide his modesty as he mounted the scales. 184 lbs: a pound under. I was surprised. Reid looked shocked. His late arrival and strip show suggested that he thought he was a lot tighter.

After he'd got his pants back on, Alex posed for the photographers. He asked them all which papers they were from and couldn't do enough for them. The flashes brought him to life. All the other fighters had held a pose for a few seconds then got off. Alex treated them to a routine lasting a couple of minutes: fighting stance, thoughtful, mean, hands up with a forced smile, Blue Steel. After running through his full repertoire, he thanked everybody and he was gone.

The BAMMA staff managed half hearted smiles. I feared the worst.

ACT IV

Fight day cometh. The national press had coverage of the weigh in. Well the Daily Star did anyway. Not in the sports pages; tucked away on page eight amidst the other celeb stories. They ran a topless photo of Alex and went for the angle of Tom being furious at his disrespectful behaviour.

I checked the Birmingham Mail to see how much hype this mega event was getting locally. Not a sausage, although Alex was name checked in a small piece publicising a personal appearance his wife was going to make at the Horse of the Year Show the following month at the NEC. Nothing in the Sports Argus pullout either. The fight of our lives didn't seem to be having much of an impact on the people of the West Midlands.

The what's on guide flagged up a rival attraction. That night, Steve Ignorant's Last Supper tour was coming to the O2 Academy. The Dagenham lad had been the lead singer of CRASS, the infamous early eighties anarcho punk outfit, and he was back on the road performing the band's best loved tunes. A highlight of any CRASS gig was the anthemic Bloody Revolutions. The lyrics explain the folly of violent insurrection and appeal for people to work together in peace to achieve real progress. They warn us that ambitious young Turks ignore historical precedent and are doomed to repeat the terrible mistakes of those they seek to replace. All of a sudden, I started thinking about BAMMA again.

It was an early kick off for BAMMA 4: doors open at four for a five o'clock start. It was all about getting the main event on TV safe and sound. The grand plan was to get Jordan's boyfriend live in front of the nation just after ten o'clock. Ripped to the tits on Blossom Hill and with a thirst for blood after sitting through the first instalment of boot camp on The X Factor, the great British public would switch over en masse to see Alex Reid. Overwhelmed by the spectacle of live MMA, they would all immediately become BAMMA kidz 4 life. The other nine fights on the card were solid but they were mere appetizers. To make sure there was no chance of them over running into the TV slot the sitting was starting early.

BLOODY REVOLUTION

I had no clue what the gate was going to be. There was no question that there would be more than had turned up at the LG in May, but how many more?

I arrived half an hour before the doors officially opened to pick up my press credentials and walked in on a comic scene. A BAMMA rep was explaining the code of conduct for the event to three photographers from the Sunday red tops. They would be allowed cageside access for all of the first nine fights (which they didn't give a fuck about) but would have to clear the area and shoot from the stands for the main event. The term 'gentleman's agreement' was bandied about. All of them nodded and said they had no intention of staying on the floor the same way teenies promise they won't sneak bottles of blue WKD into the school disco. These were the kind of lads that would defy the law, the Royal Family and all common standards of human decency to get a juicy shot. I checked to make sure they didn't have their fingers crossed behind their backs.

With a little time to kill, I hit the bars. When there's a major boxing match in town, the boozers round about are always packed. They create a temporary fight town where strangers down pints and argue the merits of the fighters. It's part of the culture, dating back to the bare knuckle days. Even when large crowds turned out for the UFC, it was something that I'd never seen replicated at an MMA event. If this was going to be the big breakthrough for UK MMA, maybe tonight was the night.

The National Indoor Arena is bang in the city. Across the canal is Brindley Place, Birmingham's attempt at an upmarket waterside leisure development. It is Anywhere UK: All Bar One, Pitcher and Piano, Pizza Express, Slug and Lettuce, Café Rouge. The full set of pubs and restaurants for people who don't really like pubs and restaurants. Chain names for chained people. There is no pre-fight buzz. There is no buzz of any kind. All the joints house the same crowd; suburban couples rounding off shopping trips and wildly unimaginative hen parties going through the motions.

Outside the NIA, I was surprised to see a crowd gathering already. The box office was doing a steady trade and close by a small band of touts were testing the waters.

- Tickets; buy or sell.

The standard grafters call. I'd never heard it at a non UFC event in the UK before. Had BAMMA pulled it off? For the first time, it dawned on me that the event may actually be a success. Even at this time, the natural pessimist inside me was nagging away.

We were in the middle of Brum and the touts were rough looking black and white lads in Stone Island jackets. They had to be linked to the Zulus. Birmingham City's firm had been going to fight shows for years. Naturally, as their raison d'être was violence at sporting events, they'd ruined a few too. Despite being home to the most impressive arena in the land, Birmingham was shunned by major boxing shows for a long time. In 1994, the Zulus and the

Salford Reds brought mayhem to the NEC during the Robert McCracken/Steve Foster British title fight. The footage of the riot was all over the telly and it was 14 years before the city staged another big fight. The Zulus were no strangers to MMA either. In May 2005, Cage Warriors put on a show in Coventry with Barrington Patterson at the top of the bill. A mob of Zulus turned out to support the local hero and went ape when he was knocked out in the first round. The disorder that followed was a major blow for the reputation of the promotion and UK MMA.

The week before BAMMA 4, there had been reports of the Zulus kicking off on a group of Welsh fans at Frank Warren's Magnificent Seven show at the NEC. Perhaps they'd got the taste for fighting at fight shows again. The Blues were at home to Wigan in the afternoon. The touts could be the advance guard and the rest of the lads may roll up when the show had got going. Or maybe the cynic in me couldn't accept there were touts around because a promoter had finally found the formula for filling an arena.

The doors opened on time; an unheard of occurrence in UK MMA. While I was getting a drink round the back, I received the most uninformative text of all time:

-Miliband elected Labour leader.

A minute later, the phone buzzed again. My correspondent had added the vital missing word: 'Ed'. Another smug white guy in a suit who'd never had a proper job had beaten his brother, two other Oxbridge educated white guys in suits and a joke candidate to win the right to debate against two more identikit white Oxbridge guys. We get the leaders we deserve. The bland leading the bland.

Walking into the arena itself was an eye opener. It was curtained off about halfway and the entire top tier was blacked out. A quick guesstimate, based on my limited knowledge of the NIA, was this configuration must hold about five or six thousand. Tickets had been priced from £15 up to £150. With this set up, it was hard to see how any seat in the house was worth £135 more than any other.

I sussed out my place. Press row was quite a few seats back from cage side. No doubt the area round the action had been reserved for people who were keen to be seen on TV.

The undercard fights went down in front of a meagre crowd. Shame because there was some quality action. Even though there were some quick finishes, the production rattled along relentlessly.

One by one, shellshocked press row veterans rolled up. Many had been caught out by not noting the early start. Others had assumed it would run on UK MMA time (an hour or two after the timings stated on promotional material).

Scott Jansen walked to the cage. A couple of rows back from me, his mates gave him a warm reception. I recognised one of the group as his girlfriend Hayley Finch.

BLOODY REVOLUTION

Hayley had enjoyed a career in glamour modelling and as a presenter on specialist TV channels. When Scott started out in the fight game, the couple got a lot of attention. There was some hopeful marketing about them being the Posh and Becks of cage fighting and it was all good fun.

Off the back of a couple of decent wins on their Contenders series, Cage Rage not only promoted Scott to their Wembley show, they put him in the main event on his debut. He was up against Pride and UFC veteran Phil Baroni, the self styled 'New York Bad Ass'. Baroni scored a crushing KO victory in the first round.

In the chaotic aftermath, Phil went over to check on his stricken opponent who was still on the floor receiving oxygen. The over emotional Jansen clan got the wrong end of the stick. Scott's brother stuck the nut on Baroni and Hayley yelled 'wanker' at the American. It was a low point that confirmed all the worst 'cage fighter' stereotypes.

At the time, the fight looked like an optimistic piece of matchmaking. With hindsight, it looks downright reckless. We had to learn from this if the sport was to move on. Surely no promotion would ever make that mistake again. Putting a fighter in a main event against a dangerous opponent just because of his relationship with a high profile glamour model; that would be madness.

Miss Finch came in for a lot of flak over the incident, even though she was a minor player in the fracas. As Scott strolled out to touch gloves with Stuart Davies, he looked composed and ready for work. A few yards to my left Hayley looked tense.

The experience that a fighter's partner goes through is not pleasant. Training burns up any spare time a man has. The food and drink you consume, both at home and in restaurants, is always an issue. Scott had moved down to Lightweight and that had to be tricky for a lad of his size, as the previous day's weigh in had proved. Most people get a little touchy when they are on a diet. When fighters are starving themselves in the run up to events that will have a huge impact on their careers, they are not the easiest people to live with.

Scott started well. He took the fight to his opponent, threw him down and unloaded some well judged ground and pound. A blink of the eye is all it takes. Stuart caught hold of an arm, threw his legs up and applied an arm bar. Scott tapped.

Hayley looked disappointed, but not overly upset. Scott had not been seriously hurt. In the life of the fight wife- that's the most important result.

There was a break so I nipped out the back for a drink. Leaning against the wall, having a pint and putting the world to rights, were Grant Waterman and Dougie Truman. Grant, best known as the Cage Rage ref, had been cornering a lad on the undercard. Dougie was one of the elder statesmen of UK MMA; the man who founded Cage Warriors. This scene of gentle cogitation was disrupted by a surreal confrontation.

BLOODY REVOLUTION

Enter stage right: Alex Reid and his trusted second Jeremy Bailey.

Enter stage left: Kong's mate John.

Fresh from his triumph as a Jordan impersonator at BAMMA 3, John had taken his act to a whole new level. He was wearing a wig of black hair full of large comedy rollers. His face was painted deathly white with black make up round his eyes to clarify the look. The outfit was some kind of black dress with a white apron emblazoned with the words: ALEX REID- DEAD MAN WALKING. His hands were shackled together with a thick chain and he was carrying a box of Scott's Porage Oats with a couple of stuffed rats in it. John was accompanied by an incredibly attractive woman. She was dressed the same as Jordan had when she was promoting her recent flop pop single; wearing skimpy black undies with her hair finned high in a Mohawk style. The lass was a bit too young and good looking to make the impersonation convincing, but we got the point.

There was a moment of hesitation as Alex Reid and cartoon Alex Reid tried to make sense of the situation. John broke the awkward silence by rattling his chains and growling:

- Alex Reid- dead man walking. Alex Reid- dead man walking.

Alex looked bewildered. Not scared- hyper puzzled. How would you react if you were unexpectedly confronted by a zombie caricature of yourself wielding cuddly rats and a porridge box? There was no logical end to the stand off.

Grant Waterman to the rescue. Grant must have some switch in his brain that is activated when he is in the vicinity of confrontation: auto-ref. He put down his drink and went into security mode. The ref stepped between the two men, puffed out his chest and gestured for Alex to come with him. Unquestioningly, Alex followed as Grant led the way to the backstage area. Undead, rollers Reid headed into the arena to cheerlead.

His entrance was a relief, drawing cheers from the crowd. They lapped up his clowning and he gave them something to focus on. With the aid of his glamorous assistant, he was providing an important public service. Boredom and alcohol are the major causes of riots and the fans were getting plenty of both as the breaks grew longer.

The only other distraction was the often repeated promo for BAMMA 5 on the big screens: Bob 'The Beast' Sapp v Stav 'Crazy Bear' Enonomou at the Metro Arena, Newcastle. To the untrained eye (95% of the audience), they looked like a fat white bloke with weird hair and a gargantuan black bloke; both of whom threw wild haymakers that made their bellies jiggle. There was so much more to them.

Stav was one of the top guys on the UK Heavyweight scene. The only blemishes on his record were a loss to Karlos Vermola and a disputed draw against Neil Grove.

BLOODY REVOLUTION

The rest of his opponents had been unable to cope with the brawler.

Sapp came to MMA via American football and pro wrestling. Reborn as 'The Beast' in Pride and K-1 Hero's, Sapp used his 380 lb frame to good effect as he bullied the much smaller opponents who were put in front of him and reached a level of celebrity in Japan that was unprecedented for a fighter. He did the movie and TV thing, charted with a CD (Sapp Time), appeared in a string of commercials and his extraordinary looks inspired an assortment of merchandise including: Bob Sapp Noodles, a Bob Sapp comic book and even a range of Bob Sapp sex toys.

All well and good but he means nothing over here. To post-Ultimate Fighter UFC fans, his name would draw a blank. The only time he may have shown up on their radar was the time he was supposed to be fighting Reidy's mate Gary Turner at Cage Rage in 2007 then left them in the lurch a couple of days before he was due in London. Hardly an encouraging precedent for BAMMA. At least the last time a celeb pulled out on them it was somebody people had actually heard of.

The North East is one of the hotbeds of MMA. If you got a couple of competitive names in a main event and filled the card with local talent, the people would turn out. Booking Sapp was about creating a spectacle, not a sport. It was 1993 all over again. From the frowns on their faces as The Beast's moobs wobbled on the screens, not many of the NIA crowd looked likely to make the trek north.

The place was filling up, but there were still plenty of cageside seats vacant when Gunnar Nelson and Eugene Fadiora got to it. This was the trade fight, the one that had most resting on it in MMA terms, yet the VIPs were giving it a swerve. Their interest in attending the event was obviously fuelled by matters other than fighting.

Gunnar confirmed his prodigy status with a slick first round sub win. The Icelander didn't break a sweat and talked about the importance of having no feelings in his deadpan, post fight interview.

In the final support bout, John Philips came forward, planted his feet and clubbed James Zikic to the floor. The Welshman looked a full weight class above Zikic in the cage. Afterwards, he called for a title shot, but the fans didn't seem arsed one way or the other. They were just waiting for the big one.

And waiting and waiting. The Bravo broadcast was due to start at ten with the main event scheduled for 10:15. That meant another ninety minutes for the restless crowd to wait. I decided to leave the great unwashed behind and check out the VIP bar. My press credential was my ticket to the land of the beautiful people. It wasn't required. With a sports jacket and a decisive walk you go pretty much anywhere in life. The security nodded as I bowled past. I was clearly a very important person.

BLOODY REVOLUTION

The astronomy of the cramped bar was clear as soon as you entered. Close to the far wall was Katie Price, wearing an lbd, matching black hair and Lily Savage eyelashes. Around her was her entourage. Next was the TV crew following her for her reality show. Orbiting the group were clusters of young women. From their heavy make up, light clothing and awe full close range gawping it appeared that they venerated Jordan as some kind of Dalai Lama figure. The outer reaches of the universe were populated by people who would slyly sneak a look at Katie, then bang on to their mates about how she was nothing special. Once that line of conversation had dried up, someone else would have a peek and the cycle would repeat. Realising I was more at home with the plebs, I left them to it.

On the way back to the main hall, I bumped into Lanus Jones and his girlfriend. Puffed up with my own self importance, I dropped the fact that I'd just come from the VIP bar. Could I get them in? Sure follow me. The three of us walked in decisive fashion into Katie-rama. Being proper fight people, we talked about the card. OK, we talked about Jordan for about ten minutes then we talked about the fights.

There had been a swing toward Alex in the days leading up to the fight. There was talk of how sharp he was looking in the gym and how he was back to his best. I'd written a preview predicting Tom to win in the first round. I accepted all the chat about Alex being a tough guy and better than his record, but he'd been away too long. MMA had moved on. Looking at fights from ten years before, when Alex was actually winning, is like watching football from the baggy shorts and laced up ball age; another sport altogether. All the things Alex had going for him: training with top guys at London Shoot, unlimited funds, Tom having a gruelling fight a fortnight back then flying the Atlantic- it didn't add up to enough to bridge the gap. Tom was as good a kickboxer as Alex ever was, he trained wrestling with GSP and Greg Jackson, had shown exceptional submission defence against far better grapplers than Alex and had the cardio to do the five rounds. The weigh in palaver suggested Alex's preparation had not been ideal and he was also coming off an injury. His leg may be healed up, but a bit of kicking and twisting will soon sort that out.

Time flies when you're enjoying yourself. Twenty minutes to fight time. As we turned to leave the bar, I spotted the only guy in there who I considered worthy of the title VIP: Steve 'Big Daddy' Bunce.

I went over to pay homage to the great man and get his take on the event. The beefy bard of boxing was everything you'd want him to be: warm, funny, outspoken and a bit pissed. Buncey's sermon for the evening was: Why can't we all get along? Unlike many boxing folk, Steve could see that the two sports could learn from each other and prosper together. The guy was singing my tune. I could have listened to him all night, but there was a fight to watch.

In the arena, there was tension in the air. It was more than the standard pre-fight buzz. 'Crazy Nights' boomed out and a few people danced and clapped along. British humans were willing to openly show their fondness for KISS in public. Stuff like this can happen when you put a load of people in one place on a Saturday night and give them nothing to do except sup ale. Inhibitions were being cast aside, along with normal standards of taste and decency. This was on the verge of getting messy.

Throughout the earlier fights, small knots of supporters were vocal when the guy they had come to support had been on. Now, the whole place was coming to life.

The notion of floor seats had become obsolete. Apart from the very VIP seats behind the metal barrier, downstairs had been declared standing room only by common consent. They had been hanging around long enough. They needed something to get their teeth into.

The boos were loud and seemed to come from all corners. Jordan had entered the building. There was none of the chanting like last time, booing and general jeering was seen to suffice; plus a photo naturally. The dame took the most V of VIP seats next to the cage, surrounded by background artistes off What Katie Did Next. The live TV show was starting.

The security staff were making vain attempts to get everyone back to their seats. Eventually, they were instructed to make a tactical withdrawal and focus all their efforts on the side of the cage that faced the curtains. This was the direction the fighters would enter from, so a clear path was required. More importantly, a clear area was needed to move the boom camera around. If the camera wasn't operational, there was no point in the fighters coming out. There was no real hostility. It was like kids playing. A security guy would push a group back then, as soon as he turned his back to deal with the next lot, they would take two steps forward.

Boos filled the air again. Katie Price was being interviewed on the big screen. The former glamour model was asked her views on the fight. Despite being prompted a few times, she would not back her man to win and repeated a mantra about how anyone who gets in the cage is a champion. It was presented as light hearted banter, but it suggested something deeper. Katie Price is a brand as well as a person. Successful brands can't be associated with failure.

At ground level, the game of cat and mouse with the security continued. Up in the stands, boredom was turning into frustration. The BAMMA staff were looking worried. Time was moving on. We were already past the scheduled fight time. How long would Bravo wait for them? Who would take them on in the future if they cocked this one up? The appeals to sit down continued but no one was listening. The decision was taken to go ahead regardless.

MC Shadd Dales comes to life.

- It's Reid versus Watson, right now on Bravo television.

At last. The Kong supporters' inflatable bananas are raised and a relieved cheer echoes round the arena. The big screen comes to life with more arty black and white images of the fighters backed by tough talking voice overs. We're on hold again as they remind us and the armchair fans about the deadly rivalry they've cooked up.

In keeping with tradition, the challenger is the first to be called to the cage:

- Alex 'The Reidernator' Reid.

The loudest boos of the night blend into violin music. Two male acrobats wearing ballet tights with lightening bolts painted on their skinny torsos flick flack through the curtains. Someone reacts to their display by throwing an inflatable banana at them. Two girls in candy striped basques come out twirling illuminated hoops. Fireworks go off.

The man himself enters, flanked by showgirls with fans and a couple of blokes in bras. A vocal kicks in on the track. It is Alex growling his way through Roxanne by The Police; a reference to his transvestite alter-ego.

The crowd all get it. The majority are tabloid readers first and foremost. They boo. A few hurl abuse. Most of the people are here to watch Jordan's feller get filled in.

They want to see the mug get served up, hopefully with a side order of claret. Their prefect ending would be Alex out cold and her standing over him, wailing uncontrollably as she drips teary fake tan and mascara into his gaping wounds.

Alex is smiling as he slowly paces to the cage. His black robe shines under the lights like a diamante studded bin bag. He loves being the centre of attention. Every now and then, an inflatable banana harmlessly bounces off him.

Hundreds of small lights appear in the darkness. Punters holding camera phones in one hand and giving wanker signs with the other. Wanting to show how much they hate the celebrity culture, but also wanting a record so they can show their mates how close up they got to the celebrities they were hating.

I'm standing against the fence separating the VIPs from the plebs. Once Alex passes the barrier, he's in friendlier territory. A group of girls from Star magazine have specially printed T-shirts. They whoop at the star of the show's arrival. Alex still has an open mouthed grin. Whatever happens, he's determined to look confident.

Alex climbs the steps up to the cage. He raises his arms with clenched fists and roars. The confidence now seems forced to the point of desperation. Thousands of boos reach a crescendo.

BLOODY REVOLUTION

FREEZE FRAME: THE STATE OF THE NATION, SEPTEMBER 2010

A moment conceived by men in suits driven by profit and realised by TV execs and marketing men. Entertainment for the masses: a hybrid of public execution, celebrity reality show and binge drinking. The chance for the great unwashed to see a tall poppy chopped down live. All around are snarling faces denouncing the icons of the trash culture: the subjects of the newspaper stories they claim they never read, the stars of the shows they never watch and particularly the man whose name inspired them to buy a ticket. Reidy is the personification of all of this. Living off his spouse's ITV 2 fame, he is trying to salvage a lost career in sport. He is the bizarro Coleen Rooney.

Small pockets of resistance appear. Alex's friends and supporters nail their colours to the mast. They are joined by a coalition of the willing to go along with it for a laugh: the mag readers, the gays and the students. Those who embrace the madness as an escape from drudgery or to flex their irony muscles. It's just a bit of fun isn't it? And it is. The haters break off from their barracking to share a giggle with their neighbours. We love being in a crowd, submerging ourselves in the mass and gaining licence to be the worst we can be. Fascism without the politics. We feel the power of unity, invigorating after a lifetime brought up in a mindset of every man for himself, hiding behind battlement hedges. We unite to address the great causes of the day: stop Joe McElderry getting to number one, keep Anne Widdecombe on Strictly, free Gail Tilsley. Wootton Basset; who's he? Did he used to be in Emmerdale? Froth is serious while the serious is presented in the language of the trivial. High School Musical politics: don't trouble yourself with the boring details, just sing along: We're All in this Together.

Alex goes back down the steps for the final checks then enters the cage without his robe. He is stripped down, wearing his tight grey camouflage trunks; just like in times gone by. The arms go up again to acknowledge the abuse. The smile is gone. As he flicks out a few air punches, he looks genuinely relaxed.

- And now ladies and gentlemen, please welcome our next fighter to the cage. The champion: Tom 'Kong' Watson.

The leader of the opposition has dropped his usual all singing all dancing act in favour of a sombre approach. Tom walks purposefully to the Ultravox hit Vienna. He couldn't spell it out any more clearly. Look beyond the spin and razzamattazz and this is irrelevant in the grand scheme of MMA. Fighting Alex is a distraction I could do without. Sing it Midge.

- This means nothing to me. This means nothing to me.

BLOODY REVOLUTION

The downbeat ringwalk has calmed the atmosphere. Tom gets a decent pop when he enters the cage, but nothing special. The MC gets to work.

- The talk is over, the hype is over...Birmingham: Are you ready?

They roar back in the affirmative. The official introductions crank it up even more. The pair are called in for their final instructions from Marc Goddard. Alex stands still while Tom bounces. They touch them up then go back to their corners. The talk is over, the hype is over. There's just the three of us: Alex, Tom and the demented rabble.

A group of guys next to me are totally flipping out, shaking the barrier and screaming. They don't stand out. I start to think about the outcome of the outcome. What happens if this finishes early? What happens if one of Reidy's signature weird endings happens? Months of hype and hours of lager have whipped the mob up to fever pitch. If they feel like they've been cheated things are going to get ugly.

Like everyone else, I can't take my eyes off Alex. This is it for him; his chance to show the wider world what he's got. So far to the general public, apart from being Jordan's bloke, he's been: the crap actor, the man in his mid thirties who lives with his parents and the bloke who bangs his head. The only fight most punters have seen him in was a narrow victory over a snowman in the Big Brother house. This is his moment to prove he's a somebody.

Round one. Alex takes the fight to Tom, marching forward and throwing leather. A minute in, he catches Tom with a big left hand. For a second, Tom looks stunned and he backs up. The VIP seats erupt. From the off, a wall of shouting has been the backing track. Now the place is actually rocking. They clinch up. The lads next to me are bouncing like four year olds who have had blue Smarties injected into their eyeballs. Tom's head pops up and we see a cut over his eye. The sight of blood draws some high pitched, female screams. Next to the cage, a man in a full banana suit shadow boxes. These are crazy, crazy, crazy, crazy nights. For the first time, it dawns on me that Alex could win. Tom scores with a few nasty elbows inside but, when they break, it's Alex landing the more eye catching work.

The end of the round and the roar turns into cheering, clapping and stamping. The lad next to me seeks my considered opinion.

- Reid innit. Fucking Reid won that.

I nod. In VIP land, 'Bad Boy' Bailey is having a blazing row with a few banana wielding Kong fans.

Round two. Alex is still coming forward, throwing straight punches down the pipe, but he's not quite in range. On the back foot, Tom is picking him off. The pace is relentless. Against the fence, an untidy takedown sits Reid on his arse. The handful left in their seats jump up. Alex stays cool and manages to push his way back up. He eats a knee to the chin, then a couple of solid punches.

BLOODY REVOLUTION

Reid drops his hands to showboat but no one is buying his act. Tom lands two unanswered head kicks to close out the round.

In the corner, Alex is smiling. That's always a bad sign for a fighter. When they laugh things off you know they're hiding something. I'm already thinking of the shape of the write up. Being stopped in the third is no disgrace. Alex was brave and flattered to deceive early but he paid for not living the life. He was never going to make the championship rounds.

He's still grinning when he comes out for the third. Alex has given his all and he's come up short. In Brazil, they have a term for the moment when a fighter realises he is in an impossible position and decides he's not going to take any more. They say he asks for the bill. Alex looks like he's smiling at the waiter.

Alex comes forward again. Tom doesn't jump on him. I'm reminded of his imperfect preparation for the bout. Maybe the Taylor fight is catching up with him. Alex makes the most of the lull. He starts showboating: dropping his hands and wobbling his legs. Tom lands a right hand. Alex calls him on. A knee drops Reid to his knees, Tom follows him down. Everyone senses that this is it. Alex hangs on in there, and eventually manages to scramble back to his feet. He's staying for pudding after all. Reid fires back, but he looks weary. He's open mouthed, cut and bashed up. No way does he get past the fourth.

Referee Goddard is sorting out the cageside chaos. Instead of the allowed three in a corner, it seems the entire front row have been up giving advice. The championship rounds loom. Alex has never seen a fourth round before. He's getting picked off and gives little in return. Still he trudges forward. Halfway though the fourth, Tom hands him off. Alex dabs his eye with his glove and raises his hand.

- Fuck off.

The volume of my involuntary expletive even shocks the psycho next door. I raise my hand to let him know I don't mean him. It's Black Saturday for all the credit Alex had accumulated in the first three rounds. He's claiming an eye poke. Another bullshit end to an Alex Reid fight. The ref isn't having it and they fight on. No whining from Alex. His stock rebounds as he digs in, but he's on the wrong end of everything. The horn sounds and Alex is already in his corner. He looks a little boy lost as he waits for his team. They hold him up physically and pump him up mentally. He finds his smile disguise again.

- Ladies and gentlemen, this is the fifth and final round.

Both fighters raise their arms. The ovation they get is like nothing I've ever heard in my life. On the scorecards, Alex Reid must be a dead man walking; his only chance is landing a bingo punch and he's shown no sign of having one in the locker. Who cares though? The wave of hostility that greeted him has been transformed. We love these guys. They've fed me and the other 5,000 with everything they've got and now they're coming out for more. They meet in the middle to touch them up and the decibel levels reach new heights. It's tear jerking stuff. Imagine the end of 'It's a Wonderful Life', but at any minute, someone could come in and ruin Christmas by caving James Stewart's head in.

Tom comes out firing, landing hard with punches and knees. He measures a crushing knee in the Thai clinch. Alex staggers back unsteadily. He's ready to go. My mind goes into fight fan mode. I want to see him knocked out. I can rationalise this. Alex is a fighter and a showman- it's the glorious way out. Also a KO is a clean and fast end. It ends the punishment and puts a full stop at the end. There's no room for the histrionics that can follow a ref's stoppage or a decision. Reflex moaning can leave a sour memory of an otherwise pleasing fight. From nuclear attacks to playground scraps, fighting maintains a pecking order and the more decisive a finish is- the less room for debate there is.

With his man on the hook, Tom shoots for a takedown. I want to slap him with a wet fish. He has him stacked up against the cage but can't find the clean shots to end it. After some untidy grappling, they are on their feet with a minute left. Alex is being urged to come forward, but he is running on empty. Less than thirty seconds to go. In the clinch, Tom's head slips down and Alex slides a forearm under his neck. He's got the standing guillotine sunk in. Realizing it's his last chance, he drops to his back and pulls guard. Alex's supporters go wild, believing he's going to score the last minute winner. The three lads on the barrier are going apeshit.

- He's fucking got it. Fucking Reid. Fucking got it.

I really want to be one of the crowd and share the excitement, but I can't. He's only managed half guard so he will struggle to get enough traction. Not to mention that the guillotine is the most energy sapping submission and Alex couldn't even hold his hands up a minute ago. The seconds tick by. With each one that passes, I question my certainty. I want to believe that Reidy can do it.

Ten seconds in, Tom kneels up and pulls his head out. The contest is over.

Alex and Tom give each other a quick cuddle. A sea of clapping hands greet them. Not a soul leaves as we pay tribute to the warriors.

Speculation about the decision starts. I say a silent prayer in the hope that we're not going to hear anything embarrassing from the judges. In a way, it's irrelevant.

Tonight was about Alex. It was his chance to show the real Alex Reid to the outside world and to prove he was still relevant as a fighter. The haters who booed him in love him now and I do mean love. There are no half measures in the fight game. No place to hide the inner you. Everyone present now knows Alex better than they know some of their family members. We saw everything Alex has in that cage. Sure there is the annoying prick who showboats a bit, but that is far outweighed by the good stuff. The guy who will never give in, the guy who carries on through extreme adversity, the guy who you'd want on your side: Alex Reid- the fighter.

This is why, from darkest Africa through Ancient Greece to the common lands of jolly olde England, we've had a fascination with nearly naked men beating the shit out of each other. Unlike other forms of sport and entertainment, it truly tells us the measure of a man. You have to trudge through all the shitty politics and sharp practice of the fight game, but at the core is the purest sport there is. It touches something inside us. Seeing two men leave it all in the cage is special. The feeling it awakens transcends the mucky marketing and the dodgy dealing. The crowd saw that and appreciated it. We love Tom and Alex. I love Tom and Alex.

In the rabble, I bumped into Dean Weir; a regular judge on the Northern circuit. He reckoned Alex had done enough to take the first two and Tom had won the rest. For me, it was 4-1 Tom and I'd argue you could have made the first even.

The official announcement comes: 49-46, 49-46 and 49-47 and STILL champion, Tom Watson. I thanked the fight gods for not making us look daft on telly. When the post fight interviews started, I checked my watch. It was well after 11. I wondered if Bravo had stuck with the show or cut it off. The fight had been the perfect intro to MMA for newcomers: competitive, minimal ground action and buckets of blood and guts.

I couldn't hear the interviews very well, but I appreciated the opportunity to cheer the lads a few more times in the gaps.

I went over and joined a motley crew of industry insiders who were discussing the night's action. The overwhelming verdict: technically shit, meaningless fight that had exposed both fighters. If you're ever on a high after being part of joyous event and you need bringing down to earth- go and hang out with people from the fight game. They'll soon knock it out of you.

BACK TO THE FUTURE

UFC 120
October 16th 2010

Jimi's dystopian interpretation of Star Spangled Banner morphs into U2's Bullet the Blue Sky. A fair chunk of the 17,000 fans in the O2 Arena start booing. An odd choice of walk in tune: a wailing condemnation of the barbarity inspired by US imperialism in the Reagan era. I suppose it's a case of whatever floats your boat.

The abuse wasn't politically motivated or a manifestation of the understandable emotion of Bono hate. It's just the kind of pantomime jingoism that goes with any international sporting event.

Cageside, the reception for Carlos Condit is more polite. The UFC pulls real celebrities. A few minutes earlier, Jude Law, Robert Downey Jr and Brazilian jiu jitsu brown belt Guy Ritchie had been flashed on the big screen. The biggest pop of the night went to WBA Heavyweight champ David Haye, another boxing guy who wants to give peace a chance.

A couple of other guests don't have their privacy invaded by the TV director. Alex Reid and Katie Price are not deemed worthy of a captioned close up. Alex has just seen his fellow London Shootfighter John Hathaway suffer his first professional loss. Hathaway was given his start in the sport by Sol Gilbert, the man who introduced Katie and Alex.

There has been mixed news for the Brit's on the undercard. Paul Sass scored a first round victory on his UFC debut- submission by way of triangle choke. His all action grappling display will earn him the $60,000 submission of the night bonus. Rob Broughton also got the W in his first fight on the big show. His M-1 England team mate Tom Blackledge had been due to make his bow too, but had been forced out by injury. The Wigan lad was scheduled to face James McSweeney. His replacement, Fabio Maldonado stopped McSweeney in the third. It took James' record in his last five fights to 1-4.

Condit is up against the UK poster boy: Dan Hardy. The Outlaw is hoping to make it a double for Team Rough House. Two days earlier, Jimmy Wallhead had finally made it onto a Bellator card. He put in an impressive performance against Ryan Thomas in Kansas City to earn a unanimous decision and a place in the 2011 Bellator Welterweight tournament.

Not every Englishman is baying for Condit's blood. Following the American is his loyal team mate and cornerman for the night Tom 'Kong' Watson. With his baseball cap pulled down, he barely attracts a glance. Surprising really. His scrap with Alex drew over half a million viewers- a massive number for a Bravo show and unheard of for MMA in the UK. The fight had been all over the tabloids, mainly going for the factually accurate but misleading line of 'Jordan's boyfriend takes one hell of a beating'. For the first time, my mum wanted to talk to me about a fight I'd covered, but she showed little interest in buying a ticket for Bob Sapp at the Metro Arena.

Dan and Carlos throw simultaneous left hooks. Condit's reaches its target first and it's all over. A stunning finish. Hardy is gracious in and manages to get a laugh in his post fight interview. Dan will be back. In a couple of years, he's gone from Donny Dome to being the face of UFC gear in the Argos catalogue and there are plenty of big fights left in him.

The result is not ideal for the UFC, but it's only a hiccup. The promotion is so firmly established it doesn't really need a local hero. Despite what was perceived as a weak card, the O2 is sold out. The brand sells the tickets, not any fighter in particular. Across town at Earls Court, the UFC fan expo has been packed with people wanting to get close to the biggest names in the sport, a lesson in marketing and promotion. To many fans, the UFC is not the biggest name in the MMA, it is MMA. Pretenders come and go, but for the foreseeable future, the UFC are the only superpower.

In the week before the fights, clues were given on the future direction of the promotion. Dana White addressed the Oxford Union and gave his familiar thoughts on the boundless potential of fighting as mass entertainment. Destinations identified for future shows included Italy, Scandinavia and India. The UK will remain a priority, with plans for four UFC shows a year and possibly more in the way of smaller fight night cards. The grand plan is audacious; nothing less than world domination.

All empires fall in time but, in the MMA world, the UFC appears untouchable. No matter what plans are being made by Englishmen in suits or tight T-shirts, they are not masters of their own destiny. In the short term at least, the future of the sport in the UK is bound up with the fortunes of the invaders from over the water. If they get it right, the prophecy will come true. MMA: the fastest growing sport in the world will eventually become massive in Britain.